A Pragmatic Approach to Chronic Disorganisation and Hoarding

Using the DESIRE Method

LINDA FAY

Foreword by Christiana Bratiotis

Jessica Kingsley Publishers
London and Philadelphia

First published in Great Britain in 2025 by Jessica Kingsley Publishers
An imprint of John Murray Press

1

Copyright © Linda Fay 2025

Foreword copyright © Christiana Bratiotis 2025

Poem on page 6 is reproduced with kind permission from David Woods.
Figure on page 49 is reproduced with kind permission from Randy Frost.

A CIP catalogue record for this title is available from the
British Library and the Library of Congress

ISBN 978 1 83997 902 6
eISBN 978 1 83997 903 3

Printed and bound by CPI Group (UK) Ltd, Croydon, CR0 4YY

Jessica Kingsley Publishers' policy is to use papers that are natural,
renewable and recyclable products and made from wood grown in
sustainable forests. The logging and manufacturing processes are expected
to conform to the environmental regulations of the country of origin.

Jessica Kingsley Publishers
Carmelite House
50 Victoria Embankment
London EC4Y 0DZ

www.jkp.com

John Murray Press
Part of Hodder & Stoughton Ltd
An Hachette Company

The authorised representative in the EEA is Hachette Ireland,
8 Castlecourt Centre, Dublin 15, D15 XTP3, Ireland (email: info@hbgi.ie)

For India who

leaves a little bit of rainbow wherever she goes

Mama Bear Loves You

ALL IS NOT LOST

BY DAVID WOODS

What kind of stuff do you hoard in your house?
Is there room for you, or not even a mouse?
Can you do those things that are of need
Or does the hoard live, move and bleed.

Across the floorboards and out of the door,
Not a great sight, in fact an eyesore,
Can you still have a bath and a cup of tea?
Or is there just stuff, is it all you can see?

Stuff on the bed and stuff in the bath,
Do you feel that the stuff's just having a laugh?
Insulting and cackling with each big old pile,
When you're frustrated the stuff gives a smile.

'Cause it's living and breathing and spreading around,
Going from nothing to a great blooming mound,
Don't feel ashamed or take on the stigma,
It's a bit of a puzzle, quite an enigma.

There's help if you want it – just hold out your hand,
And against all the stuff together we stand,
Remember that you are never alone,
Send out an email or pick up the phone.

There are many like us who face it each day,
Learning to live with it in each different way,
The task is to lighten the way that you feel,
Taking the time that's needed to heal.

So don't feel down as if all is lost,
No longer by stuff to be haunted or bossed,
Keep this in mind and read this book,
Hard work and dedication from the author it took.

Contents

Part Three: Seek a Therapeutic Approach

Part Four: Implement the Planned Intervention

Part Five: Review and Establish Ongoing Support and Maintenance

A Note From the Author

Sadly, not too long after my manuscript went into production, I had to make the very difficult decision to close Life-Pod, due to significant financial challenges. However, I am pleased to say that Hoarding Academy remains operational, and you can access the resources mentioned in this book by visiting hoarding.academy/resources.

As an eternal optimist, in my endeavour to turn a negative into a positive, I have decided to continue my learning by undertaking an MSc in Behaviour Change at Aberystwyth University in Wales, UK. This will be my first experience of further education and I'm very much looking forward to it. I have a track record of doing things slightly skew-whiff – most people tend to study and then write a book – so perhaps I'll graduate and then write another one!

Foreword

It seems impossible that for nearly 20 years I have focused my scholarly pursuits and direct clinical and community practice efforts on hoarding behaviour. I am more committed today than I have ever been to advancing scientific knowledge of hoarding as a complex private mental health problem and to innovating best practices for compassionate, collaborative, evidence-based hoarding interventions.

It is an embarrassment of riches to have an enormously sized pile of professional joys collected over many years in this field. Rising to the top of the heap are the people I've met, and the relationships I've established. Spending time with talented, committed and passionate professionals with their unique skillsets and educations, and who hail from all corners of the world, has enriched my professional and my personal life. Those who work alongside people who hoard are some of the most creative and dedicated, focused on promoting health and wellbeing and providing support so that people can live a life that is satisfying and safe. Linda Fay is one of these professionals.

With years of direct practice experience, business acumen, a curious mind, open heart and commitment to easing the way for fellow travellers, Linda developed the DESIRE approach for supporting someone who hoards to contemplate and manage their hoarding behaviour. Through this practical, easy-to-read book, Linda meaningfully contributes a hoarding resource for professionals, family members, friends and other natural supports. The DESIRE method makes use of the latest established evidence, skills and techniques combined with case examples and recommendations from Linda's client-centred, accompaniment-focused practice experience.

Each page of this text offers concrete suggestions for techniques that can be implemented today; this is a sorely needed and incredibly useful compendium. At least equally important as the content itself, this volume offers a perspective, a stance, a mindset that promotes client self-efficacy and collaborative decision-making, and centres empathy and a strengths-based approach to supporting people who hoard. One section of the text where this is on full display is titled 'Courageous conversations' (see Chapter 31). It exemplifies the everyday approach used by Linda and her colleagues at Life-Pod and is shared in a spirit desirous of respectful, productive efforts to manage hoarding behaviours.

From initial assessment to post-intervention change measurement, individual support to policy advocacy, Linda inspires professional reflexive practice that leads to a kind, thoughtful and flexible implementation of now well-established intervention techniques. *A Pragmatic Approach to Chronic Disorganisation and Hoarding* is a practical resource that is sure to be taken from your bookshelf for both careful reading and quick reference time and again. Thank you for gifting this book to us, Linda. From it, we draw inspiration, hope and help.

Christiana Bratiotis PhD, MSW,
Associate Professor, School of Social Work,
The University of British Columbia

Acknowledgements

I would like to express my thanks to Heather Matuozzo for providing the spark that ignited my passion for working in this field.

Also, David Woods, whose warm heart is as big as his brilliant brain and whose extraordinary intellectual and creative abilities astound me; his help in raising awareness of hoarding has gone above and beyond, and I couldn't wish for a better person to share a 'live' TV experience with.

Thanks to Pat Hoey for stepping out of retirement very briefly to impart a small fraction of his knowledge and expertise on environmental health-related risks and issues in Chapter 13. Pat's belief in me and my approach went a long way (further than he would believe) to helping me achieve my vision.

I would like to express my admiration for the very unassuming firefighter, John Gray (now retired from service), and my thanks for his support and encouragement.

My role at Life-Pod requires me to communicate and work with many social care professionals but Diane Elliott, the first social worker to contact me more than a decade ago, was instrumental in paving the way for Life-Pod to be recognised as a local authority specialist service provider, for which I am indebted to her.

I am grateful to each and every one of the 'peas' in my 'pod' for being a wonderful team of specialist practitioners who may be following in my footsteps but do so in their own unique way, and Richard Ibbotson for acting as my 'anchor' when I need to explore options and make decisions, which he does with remarkable sangfroid while also meeting his many other commitments, including the Autism Network and his art.

Also, my friends and family, including the 'Four Walls': Ian, Judith, Alan and especially Jack (my partner and load-bearing Wall) for wholeheartedly welcoming me into their family. My 'big' sister, Annie, my niece, Finlay, my nephew, Jed, and my beloved daughter, India.

My grateful thanks to Jane Evans at Jessica Kingsley Publishers for commissioning my manuscript and demonstrating a great deal of patience and perseverance during my first foray into writing.

Words cannot express how honoured I am that Dr Christiana Bratiotis has contributed the foreword to this book, and that Dr Randy Frost took the time to read my manuscript and provide his approval.

Last but not least, thank you to my incredible clients who amaze and inspire me with brilliant and creative ways to cope through sharing their homes with an abundance of stuff. You have made me laugh. You have made me cry. I have felt downright indignant on your behalf at the sheer injustice of the way some of you have been treated by others. But we give and receive hope for a future where society is more understanding and less ignorant to the plight and complexities of some human behaviours.

Terminology

Clients are people who use our specialist services to receive help and support for extreme clutter-related health conditions, specifically hoarding disorder.

Helper is a generic term used to describe anyone providing help and support to a person with lived experience of hoarding disorder or chronic disorganisation.

Lived experience refers to having first-hand experience with mental health conditions; 'lived' differentiates working experience from personal lived-through challenges.

Related professionals are people from multi-agencies and multi-disciplines, including emergency services, environmental and public health, housing, health and social care.

Wellbeing refers to a person's moral welfare and overall state of physical and psychological health and happiness.

Preface

Until 2012, I had enjoyed a long and successful career in corporate internal communications, focusing on change and engagement, but after 20 years in the utilities and finance industries I wanted to do something different, and specifically, I wanted to work directly with individuals on a more personal level.

I have always been a people person so, together with my communication, planning, organising and coaching skills, it felt like a natural transition into 'professional organising'. However, it wasn't long before I realised that, for some people, reorganising or letting go of their belongings was difficult and often distressing. I began research to help me understand why this might be the case, which is when I discovered and became a member of the Institute for Challenging Disorganization (ICD).

In 2013, I set up Life-Pod with the specific aim of providing practical help and therapeutic support for people whose lives were affected by extreme clutter and disorganisation. Life-Pod is a social enterprise Community Interest Company[1] (CIC, pronounced 'see-eye-see', or colloquially, 'kick'). CICs are non-profit organisations that are regulated by an officer appointed by the UK Government Secretary of State.

In 2015, after a period of study with the ICD, I passed my exams and became the UK's only practitioner to hold Specialist Certificates in Chronic Disorganisation and Hoarding Disorder. On reflection, it's fair to say that I had launched myself a little naively perhaps into the industry, but I have never looked back. As the saying goes, 'every day's a school day' and, at Life-Pod, every day is different since every client and their circumstances are unique.

At the outset, I hadn't considered developing and delivering training events but the more I learned, the more I wanted to share because I was

---

1   Community interest companies: www.gov.uk/government/organisations/office-of-the-regulator-of-community-interest-companies.

seeing first-hand the impact that ill-informed interventions were having on people's lives. Related professionals in emergency services, housing, health and social care were increasingly asking me for advice and guidance and this encouraged me to deliver my first hoarding awareness training session to coincide with Hoarding Awareness Week, launched by London Fire Service in May 2015 and supported by Heather Matuozzo and Cherry Rudge. Since then, my passion and commitment have intensified, with a fervour to ensure that people affected by extreme clutter and hoarding disorder receive support from helpers who recognise that extreme clutter can be symptomatic of a health condition and respond with insight and compassion. In September 2018, I organised and hosted the first International Hoarding, Health & Housing Conference, where I welcomed as keynote speaker world-renowned Dr Randy O. Frost, the Harold and Elsa Siipola Israel Professor of Psychology at Smith College, Northampton, Massachusetts. Sharing the stage with Dr Frost was a previous client of mine, David Woods, who invited the audience to think differently about him and his collection of books and DVDs. Feedback from the event was overwhelmingly positive and participants stated they would change their practice based on what they had learned, not just from clinicians, but importantly also from David.

In 2015, the British Psychological Society published *A Psychological Perspective on Hoarding* (Holmes, Whomsley & Kellett, 2015), which contained a recommendation that 'Everybody working with people who hoard should have access to training and information about good practice to ensure competence in the assessment of and interventions for hoarding.' I wholeheartedly agree, which is why in October 2021 (later than originally planned due to the Covid-19 pandemic) I launched the Hoarding Academy to provide an independently accredited learning pathway in the UK for hoarding disorder and chronic disorganisation. I am determined to create a standard of professional practice that inspires confidence as well as an ability to provide the correct level of help and support for everyone who needs it, which is why I have also called on government to create national guidelines for hoarding disorder.

A Pragmatic Approach to Chronic Disorganisation and Hoarding complements the Hoarding Academy training courses; it is the book I wish had existed at the start of my career in this field. It is a culmination of my skills, knowledge and experience gained over the last decade. It is also my attempt to help reduce any harm caused by helpers of people with extreme clutter since I all too often bear witness to some misguided, and dare I say unprofessional and sometimes harmful, interventions.

I describe myself as a pragmatic realist. What I mean by this is that I accept a situation as it is and deal with it accordingly, while applying a sensible and sensitive approach. Along with my team at Life-Pod, we are dedicated to helping people live safely and more comfortably in their homes. Our method is *wholistic* – no, that's not a 'typo', it's a deliberate inclusion of a 'w' to emphasise wholeness as echoed in Aristotle's philosophy that 'the whole is greater than the sum of its parts'. This underpins Gestalt psychology, which is a school of thought that looks at the human mind and behaviour as a whole – meaning we look at the bigger picture of a client and their circumstances and not just the clutter. We help people to understand their reasons for acquiring and saving stuff. We also advocate on their behalf to minimise any additional potentially harmful experiences such as enforced clearouts or risk of homelessness due to a breach in housing tenancy agreements. Collectively, we have experienced lots of funny, sad, intimate, interesting, weird and wonderful moments with our clients, some of whom have kindly given permission for me to share their stories with you, as well as some of their creative work, such as David's poetry.

I'm not a housing, health or social care professional, nor am I an academic or clinician; I am merely a human being who wants to help others in the best way I can – with compassion and without judgement. I came into this field with no preconceived ideas or boundaries, and perhaps a quixotic disposition, which has thus far served me well.

I've lost count of the number of times I've been told by people I've helped that I gave them hope; it is truly humbling, and I feel privileged to have met and worked with every single one of them. My hope is that you find this book useful in your endeavours to help people too! I invite you to bring your fervour to the fore and consider people and their clutter in a non-judgemental and compassionate way.

Introduction

When it comes to people-related health and wellbeing matters, I don't think a 'one size fits all' approach can be applied but I do find it helpful to have a framework to guide my practice. With that in mind, I created DESIRE – a method that incorporates research, evidence-based therapies, strategies and techniques with skills, knowledge and experience, producing what I hope you will find is a helpful way to appraise an extreme clutter situation and decide on the best and least harmful course of action.

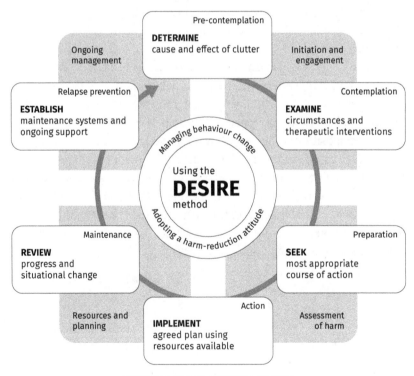

FIGURE I.1: THE DESIRE METHOD

'Hoarding disorder (HD) is a progressive and chronic condition and studies suggest an estimated 1 in every 40 adults has lived experience of problematic hoarding' (Steketee & Bratiotis, 2020, p.2). HD symptoms appear to worsen with age, and rates of HD 'appear to increase by approximately 20 per cent with every five-year increment in age, beginning in the 3rd decade of life' (Cath *et al.*, 2017, p.252). HD is also highly comorbid[1] and co-exists with many other conditions, including depression, bipolar disorder and schizophrenia. People with lived experience of HD 'have a much-reduced quality of life, a similar level of work impairment to individuals with bipolar disorder and are significantly more likely to report chronic and severe medical concerns than the general population' (Archer *et al.*, 2019, p.159).

Neurodivergent disorders (NDs) can also result in problematic clutter and lead to chronic disorganisation (CD). With the exception perhaps of attention deficit hyperactivity disorder (ADHD), research relating to hoarding and neurodivergence (particularly in adults) is very limited. One study (Goldfarb, 2021, p.1457) found through semi-structured, in-depth interviews with autistic adults aged 18–55 that hoarding behaviours were 'motivated by a need for emotional aids, disposing difficulties, and collecting items related to special interests'. Other research (La Buissonnière-Ariza *et al.*, 2018, p.4172) found that 'around 34 per cent of children aged 7–13 with autism spectrum disorders were reported to have moderate to severe levels of hoarding behaviours'.

I have structured this book to reflect the methodical stages involved when helping people affected by extreme and problematic clutter. Part One focuses on the importance of determining the root cause of clutter and whether it is a consequence of hoarding or neurodivergence, for example, autism spectrum disorder (ASD), ADHD, or obsessive-compulsive disorder (OCD). This book is neither a clinical guide nor diagnostic tool; it is a guide written by a specialist practitioner based on research, skills, knowledge, and more than ten years of experience gained in the field. Incidentally, not all people seek or want a clinical diagnosis and it isn't a prerequisite to accessing help and support services. The main benefit to identifying behaviours and characteristics of the conditions is that it can be useful to better understand people's thoughts and beliefs about their belongings and provide guidance on the best ways to

---

1   'Comorbid' is a medical term describing the presence of more than one illness in one person.

help. As well as posing potential health and safety risks, extreme clutter can be a barrier to a person receiving essential care at home. It can also affect their relationships, employment, and housing status, so Part Two includes several different assessment tools that can be used to identify and prioritise risks and issues.

Part Two also explores the individual's personal circumstances to gain a wider understanding of the problem before considering the most appropriate therapeutic interventions. We look in detail at the Model for Understanding Hoarding Disorder (Frost & Hartl, 1996; Steketee & Frost, 2003), as well as exploring evidence-based treatments such as motivational interviewing and cognitive behavioural therapies. Since we know that 'people start to work on their hoarding problem when the reasons for change outweigh the reasons for not changing, and not a minute sooner' (Tolin, Frost & Steketee, 2014, p.36), we will also look at the Transtheoretical Model (Stages of Change) (Prochaska & DiClemente, 1983), which illustrates the different stages we go through when seeking to modify our behaviour. Awareness of a person's readiness to change will help to create an individualised plan of action. Once you have assessed the severity of the situation and you have learned more about the person – their health and wellbeing, relationships, vulnerabilities, beliefs about their belongings and any cognitive processing difficulties they may have – you can start to consider the different steps that could be taken to help manage the situation.

All too often, the 'go-to' solution to dealing with excessive clutter is to carry out a clearout (enforced or otherwise) of a person's home. However, the reality of clearouts creates more problems than solutions since they address only the symptom of the condition rather than the cause. In addition, enforced clearouts create significant distress to the client, leaving them with feelings of hopelessness and despair. I believe clearouts should be carried out as a last resort and should only be considered in extreme circumstances, for example where there is a considerable safety, environmental or public health issue. In Part Three, we consider more humane and less harmful courses of action to help people reorganise and let go of some of their belongings, but – spoiler alert – they require time, patience and compassion. However, I can assure you that if you invest in helping people to understand their reasons for acquiring and saving, it will yield far better results in the long term. I cannot overstate the importance of taking the time to build trust and develop a good rapport with a client in advance of any major decisions being made, or action taken.

Part Four focuses on implementing a plan and ways you can work with the client to create SMART[2] goals and intervention outcomes, once a decision has been reached about the best course of action. An important factor that should remain central in everything we do is to focus as much on what our clients want and helping them to achieve their desired outcomes as we do in resolving problematic clutter-related risks and issues. This is fundamental to creating lasting change, as focusing only on one part of the problem will cause it to re-emerge and bring new problems into view. Be realistic about the length of time needed to implement the plan and consider where the client is in terms of feeling ready and able to make the necessary changes. We will also explore strategies you can adopt to help motivate the client and help them to identify and change unhelpful habits to achieve their goals and maintain newly acquired skills and behaviours. The skills and techniques you apply during this stage will be determined by what you learned about the client and their situation, as covered in Parts One and Two, especially whether they are affected by either a hoarding disorder or a neurodivergent disorder, as this will inform which tools and methods are best suited to the client's needs.

The process of behaviour change can be lengthy – months rather than weeks – and while you may need to quickly resolve some urgent risks and issues, remember to pace yourself and prepare for the journey ahead. Although I would encourage you to continuously review progress with your client, in Part Five we look at ways to review progress by carrying out a formal review based on goals and outcomes previously established. Doing so allows both you and the client to assess the current situation and discuss what worked as well as what didn't work so well and, going forward, what you might want to do differently. Take time with your client to reflect on what they've achieved, regardless of how big or small the changes are that they've made. There's a Chinese proverb that says: 'One step at a time is good walking.' Even if it feels as if they're meandering; sometimes it may be necessary to step back, step out, or even step away for a while, and that's okay! Also use this as an opportunity to share progress, if appropriate, with related professionals and your client's loved

---

2   SMART is a mnemonic acronym, used to set goals and objectives for better results. George T. Doran first used the term in the November 1981 issue of *Management Review* when he suggested that goals should be specific, measurable, assignable, realistic and time-related.

ones. When goals are reached it's time to celebrate. Don't be tempted to miss this opportunity; it's both a reward and a motivator to keep going.

Part Five finishes with ways to ensure that your client can independently maintain any new systems created and/or that they have support in place to help them to manage these on an ongoing basis. Since HD/ND are chronic conditions, this is vital for long-term success. Backsliding is likely with any behavioural changes and making sure clients know this may happen will help to alleviate any feelings of failure they may experience. Having established systems in place will make it easier to re-establish newly acquired habits, and being reminded of their vision for their future will help to keep your client focused and motivated to reach their goals.

DESIRE is a method to support your practice. While I hope that adopting this method will make the tasks easier, it will by no means be easy. We're asking a lot from people, and some related professionals and a client's loved ones have high expectations and preconceived ideas about what is an acceptable amount of clutter in a home. This method supports objectivity when assessing the level of clutter and identifying associated risks and issues. It allows us to remove our own standards and judgements to focus specifically on a person's health, safety and wellbeing. In essence, what we're trying to establish is a trusting, mutually respectful and therapeutic working relationship to support sustainable behaviour change.

So, if you're ready, roll up your sleeves and let's get stuck in!

DETERMINE THE CAUSE OF CLUTTER

LEARNING OBJECTIVE

After considering Part One, the reader will be able to describe and compare the key health-related causes of extreme clutter as defined in international diagnostic manuals and current clinical guidelines.

CHAPTER 1

Managing Expectations

In my experience, one of the biggest challenges relating to extreme clutter is in managing people's expectations. I would encourage you to think about it as a problem to be *managed* rather than a problem that must be *solved* because where you see clutter as a problem the client may see it as a solution to a 'problem', which could be severe and enduring. Also, letting go of the presumption of 'normal' and instead embracing 'diverse' may help you to see a person and their circumstances differently. This, combined with the belief that everyone deserves to be treated with respect and without judgement, will provide a firm foothold from which to start assessing the situation.

While contemplating how you might manage clutter-related issues, I would also encourage you to consider whether doing little or nothing is a potentially viable option. In some situations, this may well be the best option. Try to bear in mind that the situation has likely existed for many years and, in my experience, in most cases there is no need to push the 'panic' button and rush to implement a solution until you have gathered all relevant information that will allow you to make informed decisions.

I'm not suggesting you ignore problems, risks and issues but I would like to emphasise that, more often than not, these can be managed without the need to remove a person (a move to temporary accommodation, often referred to as a 'decant') or most of their belongings from their home. Occasionally, resolving urgent matters and then adopting a strategy to monitor and evaluate the ongoing situation is all that is needed.

One of the first and perhaps most important steps is to help the client understand their own reasons for acquiring and saving, and whether the clutter is consequential to hoarding disorder or chronic disorganisation as a result of neurodivergence. The more knowledge and information you accumulate, the better equipped you will be either to provide help or to signpost other relevant health and support service providers. Let's look at these health-related causes in more detail in the next chapter.

CHAPTER 2

Hoarding Disorder

In 2013, after 'twenty years of elegant and thoughtful research' (Tompkins, 2015b, p.23) hoarding disorder was officially recognised in the Obsessive-Compulsive and Related Disorders section in the fifth edition of the American Psychiatric Association's (APA) *Diagnostic and Statistical Manual of Mental Disorder (DSM-5)*. And in 2018, the World Health Organisation (WHO) released the 11th revision of the *International Classification of Diseases (ICD-11)*, which also included hoarding as a distinct mental disorder within the category of Obsessive-Compulsive or Related Disorders. The *DSM* and *ICD* are globally recognised diagnostic manuals commonly used by clinicians to identify illnesses and how to treat them.

Although hoarding is a newly classified disorder, it is not a new phenomenon. Scientific research into hoarding began only around 30 years ago, but there are many historical references to hoarding of everyday objects dating as far back as 319 BCE, when Theophrastus, a student of Aristotle, attempted to catalogue all forms of human behaviour. Two negative character types he described were the Penurious Man and the Avaricious Man. He believed people with these character types collected and saved material possessions excessively (Rodriguez & Frost, 2023). Also, Italian writer Dante Alighieri wrote in his 14th-century epic poem *Divine Comedy* that 'spendthrifts' ask: 'Why do you hoard?' and 'hoarders' reply: 'Why do you waste?'

DSM and *ICD* tend to complement each other but they can sometimes vary slightly in their use of criteria and terminology. Director of the Hoarding Disorder Research Programme Carolyn Rodriguez believes 'having a common definition has allowed for a better sense of prevalence and is helping us to focus our research efforts' (Weir, 2020). Figure 2.1 reinforces this view since both *DSM-5* and *ICD-11* denote the same elements of hoarding behaviour as found in the pivotal research paper 'A cognitive-behavioural model of compulsive hoarding' (Frost & Hartl, 1996).

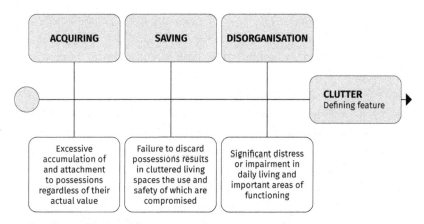

FIGURE 2.1: KEY ATTRIBUTES OF HOARDING BEHAVIOUR

HD is characterised by the excessive accumulation of and attachment to possessions regardless of their value (financial or otherwise), failure to discard possessions that results in cluttered living spaces where use and safety may be compromised, and significant distress or impairment in daily living activities (e.g. washing, meal preparation, sleeping). Clutter is a defining feature of hoarding; it is a consequence of acquiring, saving and disorganisation.

HD is a progressive chronic condition and studies (Postlethwaite, Kellett & Mataix-Cols, 2019) suggest an overall prevalence among adults of around 2.5 per cent, which means an estimated one in every 40 adults has lived experience of problematic hoarding, with an even higher frequency among older adults, since 'the disorder increases linearly by 20% with every 5 years of age – primarily driven by difficulties with discarding' (Cath *et al.*, 2017, p.252). In populations over age 55, the prevalence of clinically impairing hoarding is over 6 per cent, significantly higher than the general population prevalence (Steketee & Frost, 2003). HD affects people across all socio-economic and cultural groups and is a highly comorbid condition (around 75%) that affects men and women at similar rates.

Retrospective research suggests that symptoms of HD usually begin in childhood or adolescence (Cath *et al.*, 2017), 68 per cent before the age of 20. At ages 11–15, symptoms may start to emerge; by mid-20s, symptoms may start to impact on daily living activities; by mid-30s, symptoms could be causing significant distress and impairment; and around age 50 some will receive an intervention (Steketee & Bratiotis, 2020), but approximately one quarter of people with lived experience of HD report onset after age 40 (Dozier, Porter & Ayers, 2016) and most people affected by HD never receive any treatment for the condition.

Published papers about hoarding have increased from three during the first half of the 1990s to 319 in the first half of the 2010s (Steketee & Bratiotis, 2020). This increased rate has continued at a pace in the past few years, probably as a result of the formal mental disorder classification. Research has resulted in critical information regarding the scope and consequences of hoarding behaviours, but clinical psychologist David Tolin acknowledges that 'What we don't yet know about hoarding would fill a book' (Weir, 2020). We still have a long way to go before we fully understand the complexities of the condition.

'Possession in humans: An exploratory study of its meaning and motivation' by Lita Furby (1978) found that there are three key reasons why people acquire and save things:

1. Sentimental (emotional)

    We acquire and save objects as mementos of people in our lives, places we have visited and activities we have enjoyed.

2. Instrumental (useful)

    We acquire and save objects, including those that are broken because we think they may one day become useful or valuable; we want to explore all the reuse, reprocessing and reimagined potential to reduce waste.

3. Intrinsic (aesthetic)

    We acquire and save objects that are valuable or valued for their distinctiveness, or that we have a particular interest in.

Of course, most of us have belongings in our home for sentimental, instrumental or intrinsic reasons. Our possessions only become problematic when conjoined with excessive acquiring, difficulty discarding, and disorganisation, resulting in extremely cluttered homes with rooms having limited functional use that become unsafe and sometimes unhygienic.

The Covid-19 pandemic caused unprecedented levels of stress and fear in the general population and research has shown that those with pre-existing mental health problems experienced greater distress and negative psychological consequences as a result of Covid-19 (Xiong *et al.*, 2020), but to date there is no data on the impact of Covid-19 on obsessive-compulsive and related disorders, including hoarding disorder (Banerjee, 2020). However, some studies found associations between Covid-19 and hoarding *behaviours*, and certainly as the pandemic advanced, we saw reports in the media of people stockpiling items such as health, hygiene and food items, but as Xiong and colleagues (2020, p.1) said, 'Whether these behaviours represent healthy reactions under unparalleled stress, subclinical hoarding tendencies, or clinical hoarding symptoms, is unclear', and Fontenelle *et al.* (2021) hypothesised that hoarding-related behaviours are perhaps a method of exerting control in a situation where individuals perceive they are devoid of control. Based on my knowledge and experience in relation to Life-Pod clients, acquiring and saving behaviours were less problematic during lockdown than issues relating to being confined indoors for lengthy periods of time and increased social isolation. Many people with lived experience of hoarding are well used to not having people in their home but they do tend to spend a significant amount of time away from their home where they have opportunities to interact with others.

CHAPTER 3

Diogenes Syndrome

Also known as 'self-neglect' or severe 'domestic squalor', Diogenes syndrome (named after the Greek cynic philosopher who lived in the fourth century BCE) can be related to HD, especially *syllogomania* (hoarding of rubbish), but it can also be related to other conditions such as schizophrenia. People with lived experience of Diogenes syndrome hail from all socio-economic groups and are usually highly intelligent (Reyes-Ortiz, 2001).

Often, hoarding and self-neglect get conflated, but they are two separate conditions that don't always co-exist. If a concern is raised about self-neglect it's not unusual for an adult safeguarding enquiry to be carried out. Following this, a mental capacity assessment may be made that would then inform any decisions made about interventions. Diogenes syndrome can present complex safeguarding challenges, not least because respect for a person's autonomy must be counterbalanced by a duty of care and a need to manage resultant risks or issues.

There is no universally adopted definition for self-neglect but it is commonly described as someone who demonstrates a lack of care for themselves and their living environment, and who also refuses help or assistance from health, social care or other community services.

Described initially by Macmillan and Shaw in 1966, the term 'Diogenes syndrome' was first used in a 1975 clinical study of neglect in old age (Clark, Mankikar & Gray, 1975, p.366) that suggested the 'syndrome may be a reaction late in life to stress in a certain type of personality'. Clark *et al.* reported that from their study participants, 'Many had led successful professional and business lives, with good family backgrounds and upbringing' (p.366).

A report (Braye, Orr & Preston-Shoot, 2011) commissioned by the UK Government Department of Health and published by the Social Care Institute for Excellence documented a scoping study of the concept of self-neglect and noted that, as is the case with HD, 'cleaning interventions alone do not emerge as effective in the longer term, but assistance with daily living may be more so, particularly where self-neglect is linked to poor physical functioning'. It also states that 'building good relationships is seen as key to maintaining the kind of contact that can enable interventions to be accepted with time, and decision-making capacity to be monitored'. This has certainly been my experience – without a strong relationship you are extremely unlikely to make any lasting change.

CHAPTER 4

Animal Hoarding

Although I have been working in this field for more than a decade, I haven't personally been involved in a distinct animal hoarding situation. I have been in many homes that animals inhabited but my clients were affected by the hoarding of objects, not animals. Hence, most of the information provided here is based on my general knowledge, experience and research. But I believe that most people who hoard animals are initially motivated by a desire to rescue the animals and provide care for them, which ends up being at odds with the resulting situation.

Animal hoarding is defined by the Hoarding of Animals Research Consortium (2002, p.130) as:

> having more than a typical number of companion animals; failing to provide minimum standards of nutrition, sanitation, and veterinary care; denial of the inability to provide this minimum care and the impact of that failure on the animals, household and human occupants of the dwelling and persistence, despite this failing in accumulating and controlling animals.

A public health research report (Wilkinson *et al.*, 2022, p.5), 'Animal hoarding cases in England: Implications for public health services', found that:

> No single service or organisation has responsibility for animal hoarding and no statutory or centralized reporting mechanism exists in the UK, a position common with other countries such as North America. The incidence of animal hoarding is therefore difficult to accurately determine, but as an initial estimate the RSPCA [Royal Society for the Prevention of Cruelty to Animals], the organization most involved in welfare cases, are reported to receive approximately one thousand calls annually for multi-household animal welfare concerns and their experience highlighted that often multiple agencies are working with the same households without

32

being aware of the others' involvement. This situation is made difficult due to confidentiality and data sharing restrictions due to the Data Protection Act (2018).

Patronek (1999, p.82) described animal hoarding as 'a pathological human behaviour that involves a compulsive need to obtain and control animals, coupled with a failure to provide minimal standards of care for animals and denial of the consequences of that failure'. In his study 'Hoarding of animals: An under-recognized public health problem in a difficult-to-study population' (1999), Patronek reported findings consistent with those of Wilkinson *et al.* (2022), showing that:

> the majority (76%) [of participants] were female, and 46% were 60 years of age or older. About half of the [participants] lived in single-person households. The animals most frequently involved were cats, dogs, farm animals, and birds. The median number of animals per case was 39, but there were four cases of more than 100 animals in a household. In 80% of cases animals were reportedly found dead or in poor condition. (p.81)

He concluded his study by stating:

> This public health problem is believed to occur in every community but is poorly understood. Public health authorities should recognize that animal hoarding may be a sentinel for mental health problems or dementia, which merit serious assessment and prompt intervention. Improved cooperation between [animal welfare organisations] and public health authorities could facilitate the resolution of animal hoarding cases. (p.81)

Steketee and Bratiotis also stated:

> From a frequency perspective, most people who hoard objects do not hoard animals, but those who hoard animals do tend to accumulate excessive clutter. Both groups show strong attachment to their animals and/or objects and great difficulty parting with them. Both have limited insight (awareness of illness), although this is especially problematic in animal hoarding. Those who hoard animals are more likely to live in unhygienic conditions, neglecting themselves and others living in the home and exhibiting poor nutrition, lack of medical care, poor personal care, and social isolation. This suggests that animal hoarding may share substantial features with domestic squalor. (Steketee & Bratiotis, 2020, p.16)

A consortium of researchers and practitioners from the fields of veterinary science, psychology, psychiatry, social work and sociology worked with animal protection agencies to seek to understand why people hoard animals. The Hoarding of Animals Research Consortium (2002) suggest that animal hoarding falls into three main types (Patronek & Nathanson, 2009):

1. The *overwhelmed caregiver* who owns and cares well for many animals until a stressful life event occurs, leading them to become overwhelmed and socially isolated and there is a deterioration in living conditions.

2. The *rescuer* who undertakes to save animals from a perceived threat, fearing the animals will die and believing that only they can provide the care needed, which is often insufficient.

3. The *exploiter* who only acquires animals for their own gain and exert extreme control over the animals, showing sociopathic characteristics – lacking empathy or guilt, being manipulative and deceitful.

However, these are merely suggested signifiers and although treatment strategies have been proposed they remain largely untested. Further research is likely to be in the pipeline and it is hoped will provide more guidance for treatment interventions.

In conversation with Dr Bratiotis, she relayed the assertion (Dozier *et al.*, 2019) that animal hoarding represents a separate diagnostic group from object hoarding and suggests that this disorder deserves a new nosographic[1] category based on new diagnostic criteria, entitled 'animal hoarding disorder'. I totally agree with this pronouncement and look forward with interest to see how this develops.

In my own research, while writing this book, I discovered the article 'Noah syndrome: A variant of Diogenes syndrome accompanied by animal hoarding practices' (Saldarriaga-Cantillo & Rivas-Nieto, 2014). There is a suggestion that 'as Diogenes syndrome could be an extreme form of HD, Noah syndrome could be an extreme form of animal hoarding' (Abreu & Marques, 2022, p.53), which makes sense given that both syndromes refer to domestic squalor.

---

1   The term 'nosography' refers to the systematically written classification and description of a disease.

CHAPTER 5

Hoarding vs Collecting

Hoarding and collecting are not one and the same thing, but neither are they mutually exclusive. 'Both hoarding and collecting involve assigning special value to possessions, often value that goes beyond the physical characteristics of the object' (Frost, 2011). Collecting involves the curation of items that someone has a special interest in and enthusiasm for. People who collect objects tend to feel a sense of pride and want to talk about and show off their collection, which usually isn't the case for people with lived experience of HD.

However, it's not always as simple as it is commonly portrayed, including by the UK National Health Service (NHS 2022), which states that 'the difference between a "hoard" and a "collection" is how these items are organised'. There's also a common misconception that collectors largely save items of value and people who hoard generally save items of little or no value. On its website, the International OCD Foundation (2023) states: 'Collecting does not produce the clutter, distress, or impairment that HD does', to which I would add, until it does!

One of my clients, an 85-year-old lifelong collector who refers to his 'collectivitus', has amassed what I think is likely to be one of the largest personal collections of its kind in the world. When I first met him, none of the rooms in his home were accessible as his collection was blocking every doorway. The following case study tells the story of a kind and gentle man who has blurred the lines between collecting and hoarding behaviours.

CASE STUDY: COLLECTIVITIS

85-year-old, local authority tenant

R lives alone in the home he moved into with his family around 75 years ago. R received a diagnosis of bipolar disorder at age 55 but recalls

35

experiencing symptoms in his early childhood and saying he wouldn't go outside to play with friends because he was 'fed up'.

R was unknown to any local authority agencies until a few years ago when his neighbour contacted the housing department to ask if they could remove boarding from R's windows, which had been placed there because kids in the area had thrown bricks through the windows. This had happened on a few occasions so eventually R decided to leave the boards in situ. In response to the neighbour's request, a housing officer visited R at home and discovered there were other health and safety risks and issues that also needed to be resolved. They arranged a follow-up visit where both the housing officer and a fire officer attended and they proceeded to discuss between themselves a plan of action. At this point, all three men were stood in the entrance hallway, which is a space measuring approximately 12ft x 4ft and was the only accessible space in the home. What sticks in R's mind from that visit is the two men making the statements 'This is a fire hazard', 'We might need three or four skips' and 'I think it'll take a few days to clear it all out.' The housing officer then turned to R and said, 'I suggest you put stickers on the things you want to keep. We'll give you two weeks to do that and everything else will go in a skip.' R said, 'You can't do that – this collection is worth thousands of pounds.' The housing officer restated his suggestion about putting stickers on valuable items and then they both left, leaving R feeling understandably angry, frustrated, upset, overwhelmed and a whole lot of other emotions; he was distraught.

The housing officer made a referral to health and social care who then allocated a social worker for R. The social worker had little experience of extreme clutter and hoarding and was understandably unsure of the best way to help R, so got in touch with me to discuss possible options.

R's initial response was to give away pieces of his collection to kids in his neighbourhood but he soon realised that it wasn't going to solve the problem. A few days later he recalls 'feeling suicidal' and he started to plan his death. R withdrew all the money he had from his bank account, put it in an envelope and posted it through his brother's letterbox. He then returned home to write a letter to the housing officer and went to the local authority neighbourhood office to hand in the letter along with his house keys. Thankfully, R and the social worker met serendipitously in the reception area and R was encouraged not to surrender his house keys as this would signify resignation of his tenancy agreement. The social worker asked R if he was willing to meet with me, which he agreed to and a couple of days later we met in the cafe of a local supermarket. It is by no means an understatement to say that this meeting went on to change both of our lives in a positive way.

On my first visit to R's home, I realised he didn't have anywhere to sit, and you couldn't get into any of the rooms except the bathroom. The living room, three bedrooms and kitchen were inaccessible: boxes were stacked floor to ceiling and wall to wall, blocking every doorway. R told me it took him around 45 minutes to get into and out of his bed due to the number of belongings he had to first move out of the way. Although R thought he was 'okay' at the time with his situation, prior to involvement from the local authority the toilet had been blocked and unusable for many years and there had been no running water at the kitchen sink for 18 years, which was also inaccessible. R could take a couple of steps into the kitchen and was able to access the fridge, kettle and toaster. Although there were several health and safety issues, the risk of causing fire was minimal since there was no gas connected to the flat, which rendered both fire and cooker unusable. There were no electric heaters or other cooking facilities, and R wasn't in the habit of burning candles. However, had there been a fire, the chances of firefighters being able to rescue R in a timely manner were slim. He understood this and we agreed a plan and prioritised the first three areas to work in, namely entrance hallway, kitchen and bedroom.

On my second visit, I took a folding chair for R and he made my eyes leak when he said it was one of the nicest things anyone had ever done for him. He placed it in the hallway outside the kitchen where he could now sit to have his tea and toast.

Putting plumbing issues aside for a moment, there were no other environmental or public health-related issues in R's home. Yes, the kitchen was full, but it was mainly recycling materials. R did not like waste, so he always ate the food he bought, and he took things like apple cores outside for the birds. He kept his bathroom clear so he could use the sink to wash his dishes (using hot water from the kettle), and the bath clear so he could wash himself; he filled a bucket with hot soapy water and stood in the bath to wash from head to toe. Of course, he was unable to use the toilet but had created a routine for himself. Every weekday morning when it opened, R used the facilities in his medical practice, which was across the road from his home. At weekends, he would use the facilities in his local supermarket. R carried out this routine for years and never once did anyone in his doctor's surgery ask him who he was, or why he went there each day.

The biggest practical problem for me in R's home was lack of space and room to manoeuvre. I had little choice but to move some of the items out of the house. Luckily, there was a church nearby that was being sold so I spoke to the minister who gave permission for us to use the church hall for a period of time. It was dry, secure and in walking distance, so R agreed to the plan. Much of the collection was boxed so it was just a case of moving the boxes as they were. This allowed us to clear most of one room, which would become R's new bedroom, where he could quickly and easily get in and out of bed. The kitchen I tackled in three stages and bagged up the recycling materials and then took them in my car to the recycling centre.

On his 'up' days, R went out regularly and often met up with friends; he liked to keep active and in relatively good health and fitness. But over the months of working with R and getting to know him, I became increasingly aware of how debilitating living with bipolar disorder is for him.

When R was experiencing what he called a 'deep dip' he would completely withdraw and disengage. He wasn't receiving any regular community healthcare support and I was concerned about him so we agreed I would have a set of keys for his home so that if I visited and he didn't come to the door but I knew he was home because his key was in the door, I would leave a note asking him to remove his keys so I could get in the following day to check on him, and perhaps leave some food shopping. When R was in a 'deep dip' he spent most of his days in bed and very occasionally went out late in the evening 'under the cover of darkness', by which time local shops and supermarkets were closed. This meant that when R's medication was finished, he didn't collect his repeat prescription until he started to resurface, which would be weeks and latterly months.

With R's permission, I contacted his doctor to ask if he could approve automatic repeat prescriptions that would be delivered to R at home, and for him to make a referral for a psychiatric assessment since it had been many years (more than ten) since the last one. A few months later I received a call from a consultant psychiatrist who informed me that they intended to visit R at home and asked if I could be there; I was pleased the appointment was scheduled and more so that it would take place in R's home. However, when the consultant arrived at R's home they declared almost immediately: 'You don't have bipolar Mr R, you were wrongly diagnosed.' The consultant then proceeded to rebuke him for not being consistent in taking his medication. I was appalled at this lack of sensitivity and deeply saddened when I turned to R and saw the impact of these words on his face. He'd just been told by a complete stranger that he had been taking prescribed medication for more than 25 years that he didn't need, along with the insinuation that by not taking it he was making his symptoms worse. The consultant then asked R some questions about his mood and daily living activities and then concluded that they 'were not overly concerned' about his health and advised R to immediately stop taking his prescribed medication – both lithium and temazepam. R stated that he disagreed with them but they got up to leave at which point I asked if there was anything R could take in place of these medicines and was told they would speak with his doctor.

Unsurprisingly, a few weeks after that appointment, the key arrangement stopped working. R was struggling to come out of his 'dip' and didn't respond to my request to remove his key, so I climbed in through a small window at the back of his home and found him sitting in the dark with his coat on. He wasn't very communicative with me. I told him I was worried about him and his mental state and asked him if he would allow me to take him to the hospital for an assessment. His initial response was 'no' and he asked me to leave him alone, but I couldn't because I knew this was not his 'normal' behaviour. I explained to R the risk of him not coming voluntarily with me may lead to his doctor issuing a Section 2 notice under the Mental Health Act, which could result in him being hospitalised against his will. He reconsidered and I drove him to the hospital where he was seen by a more caring, considerate and compassionate doctor, who confirmed that the original diagnosis of bipolar disorder was correct.

Today, R still lives in a 'cluttered' home but in adopting a harm-reduction attitude, we manage his home environment by working around the challenges of his ill-health and making sure he can carry out daily living activities and easily access areas for food preparation, bathing, sitting, and sleeping.

CHAPTER 6

Neurodivergent Conditions

A couple of years after Frost and Hartl (1996) published their pivotal research on hoarding, sociologist Judy Singer first coined the term 'neurodiversity' in her Honours thesis (Singer, 1998):

> The rise of Neurodiversity takes postmodern fragmentation one step further. Just as the postmodern era sees everyone's too solid belief melt into air, even our most taken-for-granted assumptions: that we all more or less see, feel, touch, hear, smell, and sort information, in more or less the same way, (unless visibly disabled) are being dissolved. (p12)

Following on from and related to her thesis, Singer (1999) contributed a chapter 'Why Can't You Be Normal For Once In Your Life?' to the book *Disability Discourse*, which brought her work to a wider audience, including the Neurodiversity Movement.[1]

The concept of 'autism' was formulated in 1911 by the German psychiatrist Eugen Bleuler to describe severe cases of schizophrenia (Bleuler, 1950 [1911]) and this formulation was used until, in the 1960s, many British child psychologists challenged Bleuler's theories and assumptions and created new methods to validate child psychology as a science, in particular epidemiological studies. Autism was then completely reformulated as a new descriptive category to serve the needs of this new model of child development, and from the mid-1960s onwards, child psychologists used the word 'autism' to describe the exact opposite of what it had meant up until that time (Bonnie, 2013).

More recently, based on scientific evidence as well as views from people with lived experience, experts, practitioners and prominent thinkers on neurodiversity, Scotland's National Autism Implementation

---

1   The Neurodiversity Movement is a social justice movement that seeks civil rights, equality, respect, and full societal inclusion for the neurodivergent, incorporating the principles of the autism rights movement and disability rights movement.

Team published a model (Shah, 2022) and definitions of important terms related to neurodevelopmental disorders. Having developed a previous model (Shah, 2013), Shah (2022, pp.578–579) wanted to provide a new 'descriptive model incorporating the different viewpoints without regarding one as more valid than any other' and generated the following:

- **Neurocognitive** functions are selective aspects of brain functions – for example regulating, learning, attention, emotions, impulses, sensory processing and social behaviours. These traits, present from birth, may be significantly genetically influenced, the normal range dependent on age.

- **Neurodevelopment** is the process of change of these selective brain functions with age.

- **Neurodiversity** is the statistical normal range of function in a population at a particular age. Neurodiversity is a characteristic of the whole population, not a specific individual.

- The societal norm for selective **neurocognitive** functions is the range that society regards as being normal for a given age – these may be narrow, variable, arbitrary and influenced by context and culture.

- **Neurotypical** describes individuals whose selective neurocognitive functions fall within prevalent societal norms.

- **Neurodivergent** describes individuals whose selective neurocognitive functions/neurodevelopmental differences fall outside prevalent societal norms. They do not necessarily have a neurodevelopmental disorder.

- A **neurodevelopmental** disorder or condition is a term reserved for those whose neurocognitive function lies at an extreme for a given age with associated significant functional impairment.

- The risk of functional impairment increases as the **neurocognitive** function becomes more extreme, and if the environment becomes increasingly unsupportive.

- Neurodevelopmental differences describe various **neurotypes** without labelling these as disordered, divergent, or functionally impaired.

Some **neurodivergent** conditions that commonly co-exist with hoarding include autism spectrum disorder, attention deficit hyperactivity disorder, obsessive-compulsive disorder, schizophrenia and bipolar disorder as well as acquired neurodivergent conditions such as hydrocephalus, traumatic brain injury (TBI), and post-traumatic stress disorder (PTSD).

CHAPTER 7

Chronic Disorganisation

Judith Kolberg, who is credited with launching the professional organising industry devoted to addressing the needs of people who are challenged by chronic disorganisation (CD), said: 'Chronic disorganisation is a quality-of-life issue, not a medical condition' (2007, p.10). Kolberg is the founder of the National Study Group on Chronic Disorganization, the predecessor of the Institute for Challenging Disorganization (ICD),[1] and she describes CD as:

> the result of the bad fit between people who organise unconventionally and the very conventional organising methods which exist for them to use, which has three defining features: (i) the persistence of severe disorganisation over a long period of time, (ii) a daily undermining of one's quality of life by disorganisation, and (iii) a history of failed self-help efforts. (2008, p.4)

If we compare CD to other chronic physical or mental conditions, we know that often the longer an individual has had the condition the more difficult it is to treat or manage, so early intervention is beneficial. However, while improvements and adjustments can be made to alleviate some of the symptoms, the individual will always be living with and managing the condition.

Similarly, situational disorganisation could be compared to an individual who is in good health but suffers serious injuries as a result of an accident. The injuries may be severe, and the individual may need rehabilitation therapy, but with the right help and support to make modifications they will, after a period of time, return to generally good health. Table 7.1 below highlights some key differences between situational disorganisation and chronic disorganisation.

---

1   The ICD is a non-profit organisation in the USA whose mission is to provide education, research and strategies to benefit people challenged by chronic disorganisation.

Table 7.1: Situational vs chronic disorganisation

	Situational	Chronic
Onset	Abrupt	Childhood (may develop gradually)
Duration	Limited	Lifelong
Cause	Usually caused by a single event or several events within a short space of time (e.g. redundancy, divorce/separation, birth/ adoption, death or illness)	Often multiple causes and usually comorbid neurologically brain-based conditions (e.g. ADHD, ASD, bipolar disorder, dyslexia, hydrocephalus)
Outcome	With the right intervention, the situation can return to previous state	With the right intervention, improvements can be made and systems and strategies developed but likely to continue to be an ongoing challenge

That's quite a lot of definitions and descriptions I've thrown your way and I hope they demonstrate the complexities of consequential clutter and perhaps go some way to explain why enforced clearouts don't solve the problems, but we'll cover that more fully in Chapter 14. Before we get to that, the following case study explores some of the human pathology behind the diagnoses.

CASE STUDY: THE CREATOR

65-year-old, social housing tenant

An example of lived experience of chronic disorganisation can be seen with one of my clients, D, who at the age of 30 was diagnosed with hydro-cephalus[2] that required him to undergo 13 brain operations, which caused significant memory loss and he believes also resulted in him having 'acquired autism spectrum disorder'. Regardless of whether clinicians agree or disagree with his belief, I can certainly appreciate why he thinks this, given his multiple brain surgeries.

The strategies D has created for himself that enable him to live independently are quite simply astounding. Everywhere D goes, he takes with him a bag that contains several notebooks and yarn for him to knit.

---

2   Hydrocephalus is a build-up of fluid in the brain – adding pressure, which if left untreated, can be fatal.

His notebooks are filled with written details and 'reminders' and are assigned a series of numbers and letters – akin to a code that is meaningful to D. For example, some numbers relate to dates and times whilst others determine his level of stress, anxiety or feelings of happiness. D points out that he doesn't enjoy knitting but he does so because it helps him to process information and be able to focus whilst engaging in a conversation. Nevertheless, he puts his knitting to good use by creating what he calls 'friendly squares' that he gives away to people whom he feels he's had a positive connection with.

Knitting is just one of the many creative methods that D adopts to manage his health and wellbeing. He comes from an artistic family but doesn't think of himself as an artist; instead he refers to himself as 'creative'. D's home is bright and colourful due to the materials he has used to decorate it with. There's no denying that D's home is cluttered but to him the 'clutter' is a source of materials and items that he uses in his creative projects; he is extremely resourceful. He uses what most people refer to as 'rubbish' and 'junk' for selecting words and images to create a story, picture or objects d'art, albeit usually on a larger scale. If you discarded the supposed 'clutter' from D's home, you would be removing a vital part of his life that is fundamental to his coping strategies.

D can't remember what happened yesterday, or the day before, or most of the days throughout his life. He has created processes and routines that help him to live in his own individualistic way. Because he is smart and articulate, people meeting D for the first time could perhaps be forgiven for not understanding the numerous challenges he faces every single day, and even I have to remind myself not to say things like: 'Do you remember we talked about that last week?', or 'Do you remember when we went to...?' because of course he can't remember; it's not because he forgets, it's because he is unable to remember!

Part Two

EXAMINE AND ASSESS THE CIRCUMSTANCES

LEARNING OBJECTIVES

Following examination of the Model for Understanding Hoarding Disorder, it is expected that the reader will be able to identify key components and complexities of hoarding behaviour.

Subsequent to appraisal, it is expected that the reader will be able to identify the most appropriate assessment tools required to categorise and prioritise extreme clutter-related risks and issues.

CHAPTER 8

Model for Understanding Hoarding Disorder

To affirm a previous point, in order to effect change, it is vital that we help people with lived experience of HD to be aware of and understand their behaviours. Fortunately, Drs Frost, Steketee and Tolin and others have worked assiduously over the past 25–30 years to create a valuable set of effective evidence-based strategies, tools and techniques that can help us to better comprehend and assess a hoarding situation.

Originally presented by Randy O. Frost and Tamara L. Hartl in 1996, then subsequently refined by Gail Steketee and Frost in 2003, the Model for Understanding Hoarding Disorder, illustrated in Figure 8.1, emphasises how underlying vulnerabilities and deficits in cognitive processing can lead to beliefs and emotions that result in extreme clutter.

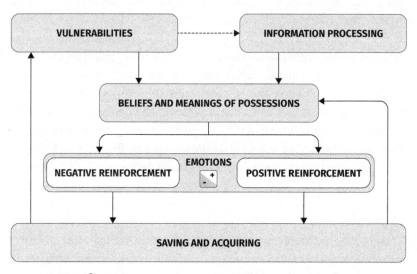

FIGURE 8.1: MODEL FOR UNDERSTANDING HOARDING DISORDER
(RECREATED IN 2019 WITH PERMISSION FROM SOURCE)

Twenty years on, Tolin (2023) has proposed the biopsychosocial model of HD, which expands on the original cognitive-behavioural model by:

> Introducing advances in neuroscientific research to help clarify some of the likely mechanisms underlying the phenomenology of HD. With its suggested biphasic abnormality in brain activity (which is not part of the original cognitive-behavioural model), the model provides an explanatory framework not only for difficulty discarding but also for the diminished insight and motivation. (p.2)

The biopsychosocial model was introduced in 1977 by psychiatrist George Engel as the bio-psycho-social-cultural model, then shortened to biopsychosocial because culture was an aspect of the social factor of the model, as well as for ease. 'Biopsychosocial' refers to medical conditions where biological (genetics, health), psychological (thoughts, feelings, actions) and social (economic, environment, culture) factors all play a significant role in our health and wellbeing (McInerney, 2002). This model was seen as a very important step in medical care and was reflected in the WHO's revised constitution of Health (1986): 'Health is a positive concept emphasising social and personal resources, as well as physical capabilities.'

As a matter of interest, the current (2023) WHO constitution states: 'Health is a state of complete physical, mental and social wellbeing and not merely the absence of disease or infirmity' and 'Mental health is an integral and essential component of health.' WHO also states: 'Mental health is fundamental to our collective and individual ability as humans to think, emote, interact with each other, earn a living and enjoy life.'

Assimilating as much information as you can in relation to these models will help you to gain a wider knowledge and understanding of a client's circumstances and help to inform any decisions made about the most appropriate type of intervention required. I would suggest you start by exploring the individual components of Figure 8.1 Model for Understanding Hoarding Disorder, as set out below.

Vulnerabilities

This component involves the exploration of a client's genetic and family history, biology, stressful or traumatic life events and co-existing health conditions. Some of these factors are not specific to HD but may make individuals more susceptible to mental ill-health.

Hoarding behaviours tend to run in families and 'gender may play a role in impacting the effects of genetic and environmental factors on the development and presentation' (Dozier & Ayers, 2017, p.296). HD is high among first-degree relatives of people who hoard and is affected by gender: more female relatives (mother and daughter) compared to male relatives (father and son) (Steketee & Bratiotis, 2020). Indeed, Monzani *et al.* (2014) suggest that all obsessive-compulsive and related disorders carry risk of characteristics being inherited by a child from a biological parent.

Traumatic life events can also make people more susceptible to hoarding. One study (Grisham, 2006) reported that 55 per cent of a sample of adults with hoarding behaviours had experienced a stressful life event before the onset of their symptoms. Others identified greater frequency and greater number of different types of traumatic events, especially having had something taken by force, being physically handled roughly in childhood or adulthood, and being forced to engage in sexual activity in childhood or adulthood (Hartl *et al.*, 2005), and significant association to childhood adversities (e.g. home break-in, physical abuse), alcohol dependence and personality disorder traits (Samuels, 2008). However, contrary to popular belief, 'there is no support for the hypothesis that HD is related to material deprivation early in life' (Frost & Gross, 1993, p.367).

Individuals with HD have a similar degree of work impairment to individuals with bipolar disorder. They also have high rates of unemployment, usually live alone, have often never been married, may have lived through a suicide attempt, and are significantly more likely to report chronic and severe medical concerns than the general population (Tolin *et al.*, 2008).

In the past 25 years or so, the majority of studies relating to HD report its high comorbidity rate, with the most common at 98 per cent being major depressive disorders (Archer *et al.*, 2019). This has certainly been my experience, but there are many other common co-existing conditions, including autism, obsessive-compulsive disorder, attention deficit hyperactivity disorder, substance misuse, fibromyalgia, bipolar disorder and schizophrenia.

Let us, for a moment, consider some of the symptoms of these co-existing conditions and how they might affect someone with HD or ND.

- **Attention deficit hyperactivity disorder** – difficulty concentrating and focusing, impulsiveness.

- **Autism** – anxious around others, don't like disruption in routines, communication and social cues can be challenging.

- **Bipolar disorder** – mood swings that range from extreme highs (mania) to extreme lows (depression).

- **Depression** – persistent low mood, feeling hopeless and helpless, lack of motivation, difficulty making decisions.

- **Fibromyalgia** – widespread pain, migraines, fatigue, problems with mental processes (known as 'fibro-fog') such as difficulty concentrating or remembering.

- **Obsessive-compulsive disorder** – distressing thoughts, repetitive behaviours, feeling intensely anxious.

- **Schizophrenia** – delusional thoughts, unusual beliefs, socially withdrawn, disorganised and unpredictable behaviour.

- **Substance misuse** – social and domestic problems, insomnia, low mood.

Information processing

Frost and Hartl's (1996) preliminary research suggested that three types of information processing deficits are associated with compulsive hoarding – (1) decision-making, (2) categorising and organising, (3) memory – and that indecisiveness is a hallmark symptom of the condition. Perfectionism, in particular the 'concern over mistakes' aspect (Frost *et al.*, 1990) (which refers to the tendency to react negatively to mistakes, to interpret mistakes as equivalent to failure, and to believe that one will lose the respect of others following failure), was also found to have a significant association with HD. This topic is discussed in more detail in Chapter 30.

A recent systematic review (Gledhill *et al.*, 2021) of the existing evidence for impaired information processing in HD concluded that the overall findings were consistent with a previous review (Woody, Kellman-McFarlane & Welsted, 2014) which suggested some impairments in attention, working memory, organisation, motor inhibition,[1] and visuospatial

---

1   Motor inhibition facilitates the development of executive functions such as thought before action, decision-making, self-regulation of affect, motivation and arousal.

learning.[2] However, Gledhill *et al.* stated that literature on deficits in other areas of executive functioning is wide ranging and limits the extent to which firm conclusions can be drawn.

Memory

Our memory works by storing and processing information, which it does in three key stages:

1. **Sensory memory** – gathering information using our five senses: iconic (sight), echoic (sound), olfactory (smell), gustatory (taste) and haptic (touch).

2. **Working memory** – processing information (including attaching meanings and beliefs).

3. **Long-term memory** – storing information (for later retrieval).

Woody *et al.* (2014) suggested that people with HD lack confidence in their own memory and overestimate the importance of remembering information, and so to compensate want to have all of their belongings in sight. It's this lack of confidence rather than any measurable impairment in memory that results in acquiring and saving behaviours. In addition, some people who hoard imagine they will suffer serious consequences if they are unable to remember certain pieces of information, and this perceived failure causes distress and anxiety. To illustrate this, I worked with a client who shared his home with a large number of books and publications, and he explained to me that he felt a strong need to gather as much knowledge and information as he could because he feared that when he dies and arrives at the 'big pearly gates',[3] he will be turned away because he is unable to answer a prerequisite question.

Decision-making

Early studies also indicated that people with HD may experience an exaggerated sense of responsibility for harm (Frost *et al.*, 1995). What I see in relation to this is some people's beliefs that their items are unique, so if an

---

2 'Visuospatial learning' refers to a person's ability to perceive, analyse and understand visual information in the world around them.

3 Pearly gates is an informal name for the gateway to Heaven, according to some Christian denominations.

item becomes damaged or lost it will be irreplaceable. These beliefs make belongings feel of significantly more value and therefore more difficult to part with. Having said that, it seems as though making the decision is by far the most difficult task and once a decision has been made to let go of something, the emotional attachment is lessened or dissipates.

A more recent study (Tolin *et al.*, 2012) in which a group of people with HD were asked to make decisions about whether or not to shred items of 'junk mail' and newspapers they had brought from home appears to confirm my observations. Participants' brain activity was being imaged throughout the exercise and showed excessive activation in the anterior cingulate cortex, a region of the brain involved with decision-making, especially in situations involving uncertainty or conflicting information. Brain activity was also raised in the insula, an area that monitors the emotional and physical states. Both of these regions help us to assign levels of importance or significance to objects.

Categorising and organising

Since each item is believed to be unique, sorting and categorising is problematic because of a desire to create a separate category for each item. As a result, due to space restrictions, new stacks of clutter are created, and a process of 'churning' ensues.

Nevertheless, it often seems as though churning gives the impression of organised chaos. I am flabbergasted by the number of clients who can tell me exactly where an object is, when they put it there and when they last used/accessed it regardless of whether they can see or retrieve it. They appear to create what I think of as a mental mind-map as a way of navigating through the various stacks of their belongings throughout the home.

In addition to uniqueness, when people with HD are attempting to organise their belongings, they often apply an equal value to objects, that can render them all 'very important'. As an example, while working with a client to sort through a pile of 'important' papers, I came across a receipt for a cup of coffee and underneath the receipt was a cheque to the value of £42,000 that should have been paid into a bank. This can be one of the reasons why people with HD become upset and anxious at the thought of piles of things being discarded without them having examined everything carefully, because there may well be something of 'real' value among it all.

Beliefs and meaning

According to Frost *et al.* (1995), people with HD 'view many of their possessions as extensions of themselves' (p.902). The possessions are part of their owner and are 'imbued with human-like qualities' (p.898). When other people touch, move, or use the possessions, the [owner] feels violated, as if they've lost control of their environment.

In his paper titled 'Possessions and the extended self', Russell Belk (1988, p.139) said, 'We feel and act about certain things that are ours very much as we feel and act about ourselves' but he acknowledged that 'the premise that we regard our possessions as parts of ourselves is not new'. William James (1890, pp.291-292), who laid the foundations for modern conceptions of self, held that:

> A man's Self (sic) is the sum total of all that he *can* call his, not only his body and his psychic powers, but his clothes and his house, his wife and children, his ancestors and friends, his reputation and works, his lands, and yacht and bank account. All these things give him the same emotions. If they wax and prosper, he feels triumphant; if they dwindle and die away, he feels cast down, not necessarily in the same degree for each thing, but in much the same way for all.

If we define possessions as things that we call ours, James was saying that 'we are the sum of our possessions'. Certainly, on many occasions while working with clients I have heard them make statements like, 'Asking me to let go of this is like asking me to lose a limb', 'This feels like it's a part of me', 'No-one else could appreciate this in the same way as I do', 'I feel responsible for this, so I need to look after it'.

Emotions

The study carried out by Frost *et al.* (1995) found that participants felt a "hyper sentimentality' about possessions, and suggested there are two types of emotional attachment to possessions that are associated with hoarding: (1) pure sentimentality – possessions were seen as a part of the self and getting rid of them was like losing a close friend, and (2) emotional attachment – possessions were providing a source of comfort and security that may signal a safe environment.

Also, things that stimulate our emotions either positively or negatively will affect how we behave. If acquiring things makes us feel good – safer and more in control – then we will want to do more of it. Conversely, if discarding things makes us feel bad – causing distress and anxiety – we will avoid doing it.

Another type of emotional attachment is anthropomorphism, which relates to when we see non-human objects as human – a common behaviour that we all unvaryingly adopt. Examples of anthropomorphism are often illustrated in mythology, books, and films such as *Cars*, [4] which features a rookie race car named Lightning McQueen and a plot that sees him learning some hard life lessons. Also, in everyday life, examples of anthropomorphism can be seen in children talking to their teddy bears, or adults talking to and naming their cars, or dressing their pets.

A psychological study (Wan & Chen, 2021) hypothesised that people who hoard show stronger anthropomorphic tendencies 'to fulfil unmet belonging needs' associated with 'enhanced perception of the objects' sentimental and instrumental value, and this enhanced value mediated the relationship between anthropomorphism tendency and object attachment'.

The study also found that stronger tendencies to anthropomorphise inanimate objects were related to greater distress intolerance and greater anxious attachment, leading to greater buying and acquisition of free items.

Wan and Chen (2021, p.89) state: 'The measures of sentimental and instrumental value capture people's need in seeking comfort and pleasure, strengthening self-identity, and boosting self-efficacy.'

Anxious attachment was born out of 'attachment theory', developed by psychoanalyst John Bowlby in the 1950s and later developed (Ainsworth & Bell, 1970; Main & Solomon, 1990) to incorporate four attachment styles, three of which are known as insecure attachment styles, of which anxious attachment is one. Clinical psychologist Sarah Bren indicated that an anxious attachment style can emerge when a child's interactions with their caregiver feel inconsistent, intrusive or overwhelming (Lebow, 2022). Wan and Chen suggest that treatment for HD that includes targets for improving distress tolerance and reducing anthropomorphism could help to reduce excessive acquiring.

---

4   *Cars* is an animated film franchise produced by Pixar and released by Walt Disney Pictures in 2006.

Acquiring and saving

On the basis that reasons to save and reasons to discard are both related to the intention to discard an item, studies (Frost *et al.*, 1998) show that people with HD provide more reasons to save an item than people without HD, but they did not give fewer reasons to discard an item. This suggests that the nature of beliefs that may drive hoarding behaviour have more to do with thoughts about saving belongings than with thoughts about why belongings should be discarded. Frost *et al.* implied that cognitive therapy should focus more on getting clients to reduce their reasons to save, rather than generate reasons to discard items.

Other research has also shown that both impairment in response inhibition (the ability to suppress actions that are inappropriate in a given context and that interfere with goal-driven behaviour) and the severity of HD increase with age (Rasmussen *et al.*, 2013), and it could therefore be argued that as those with HD age, it becomes more challenging for them to resist their urges to acquire.

Consequently, all of these factors outlined above – vulnerabilities, cognitive processing deficits, beliefs and strong emotional attachments – often leave people with HD living in homes that become unsafe and unsecure environments due to their excessive acquiring and saving behaviour, in addition to the difficulty they have in discarding items.

CHAPTER 9

Emerging Studies and Theories

Since the original publication of the Model for Understanding HD (Frost & Hartl, 1996) and its subsequent refinement (Steketee & Frost, 2003), additional concepts are being considered as relevant to the onset and progression of hoarding, and we will explore them in this chapter.

Early life stress in adults with HD

A mixed method study (Sanchez *et al.*, 2023) was carried out to clarify the specifics of the relationship between the 'mid-childhood' onset of HD symptoms and early life stress (ELS), which is a known associated feature of negative mental health outcomes. The study used qualitative and quantitative results to build on the cognitive behavioural model of HD and concluded that: 'Consistent with earlier research that people with HD experience absence of early warmth, early experiences of prolonged stress or scarcity of emotional support are key contributing vulnerability factors' (p.1). Sanchez *et al.* suggest that screening for ELS experiences is important when working with individuals with HD, and that HD treatments may benefit from increased focus on social and emotional connection.

Social cognition and intervention training

'Social cognition' is a term used to describe how we cognitively process and respond to social interactions. In general, social cognitive processes can be clustered in three domains:

1. **Perception** – processing social information including body language and facial expressions. *Example: When meeting a friend, you are greeted with a big smile.*

2. **Understanding** – decoding and interpreting information, behaviours and social rules. *Example: You assume your friend is happy to see you.*

3. **Decision-making** – considering and responding appropriately to the social situation. *Example: You say, 'It's great to see you,' and give them a hug.*

Based on suggestions from emerging research that 'hoarding may be associated with reduced social cognition, specifically reduced theory of mind and hostility biases, which may contribute to the social difficulties observed in this population', Chen *et al.* (2023) undertook a study with the primary aim to evaluate 'the feasibility and acceptability of Social Cognition and Interaction Training (SCIT) in a sample of individuals with HD and assess its potential as an adjunct to CBT; and secondarily to examine changes in loneliness and hoarding symptoms'. Results from pre-to post-treatment revealed that 'participants had an improvement in theory of mind for sarcastic remarks and a reduction in hostility bias, hoarding symptoms, and loneliness. Retention was also good as all participants completed treatment.' The pilot study concluded that 'SCIT is a promising treatment to improving social cognition for hoarding disorder and may improve interpersonal difficulties such as loneliness. We propose that SCIT may represent a potential adjunct targeting social factors to improve the efficacy of CBT.'

Sleep management and HD treatment

Recent studies investigating HD and sleep impairment found a strong link between hoarding symptoms, sleep disturbances, reduced sleep quality and daytime fatigue (Nutley *et al.*, 2022). Sleep disturbance remained significant even when controlling for the ability to sleep in one's bed, suggesting that hoarding symptoms other than clutter play a large role in sleep impairment among individuals with hoarding behaviour (Dozier *et al.*, 2021). This has led to the researchers involved suggesting that 'careful assessment and management of sleep behaviour is a critical component of hoarding treatment' (Nutley *et al.*, p.487). Nutley *et al.* concluded that identification of sleep problems among those with hoarding symptoms is a critical component of hoarding assessment and that further research is needed to better understand the mechanisms underlying the observed relationship and examine the role of sleep management in the treatment of hoarding behaviour.

Object-Affect Fusion

'Object-affect fusion' (OAF) refers to the central psychological process that helps to explain our thoughts, feelings and behaviours, and when applied to HD, individuals with lived experience seem to meld the emotions they associate with objects to the objects themselves. These concocted emotions take root and make decisions about discarding far more difficult.

In 2006, Kellett completed an initial experimental case study of an individual with lived experience of HD. The study incorporated five key stages: identification, description, cognitive challenge, affective expression and behavioural discard, and offered preliminary evidence that OAF, due to its emphasis on recognising the range of 'bonds' or 'attachments' of the person to the object, appeared to be a useful addition to CBT treatment approaches for hoarding. Kellett also reported that 'OAF was used as a precursor and primer for other CBT techniques. For each object or range of objects, a procedure was followed to identify, name and describe OAF processes' (p.11) and 'in terms of hoarding, the patient reported a new-found ability to discard of objects previously cluttering the home, a new sense of freedom in terms of abilities to re-organize her home and also to engage in activities outside the home, reducing levels of social anxiety and phobia' (p.18).

In addition, Kellet stated:

> The concept of OAF has previously been proposed (Kellett & Knight, 2003) to be particularly useful in the consideration of the sentimental form of hoarding (Furby, 1978). The employment of OAF concepts during treatment appeared additionally to also have positive effects across instrumental and intrinsic forms of hoarding (Furby, 1978). (p.18)

In the repeated absence of an adult (e.g., parent) for a child to 'attach' to, they may develop a lasting insecure attachment style that can manifest as either attachment anxiety (i.e., fear of abandonment) or attachment avoidance (i.e., fear of intimacy). For individuals with attachment anxiety, object attachment has been suggested to act as a substitute for interpersonal relationships because relationships with inanimate objects may be perceived as less threatening than with people (Grisham *et al.*, 2018). Attachment anxiety and object attachment were both shown to be significant predictors of hoarding symptoms (Neave *et al.*, 2016, p.33).

Self-identity, self-criticism and shame

Evidence suggests a link between hoarding and self-identity (Kings, Moulding & Knight, 2017; Chou *et al.*, 2018). Kings *et al.* described case reports of people with hoarding behaviour who formed strong emotional attachments with possessions that they associated with the identities of others (e.g. a deceased spouse). These possessions could similarly be associated with the person's perception of individuality (i.e. objects becoming symbols of their personal passions and interests). Chou *et al.* (2018) found that aspects of compromised self-identity (e.g. self-criticism and shame) were positively correlated with hoarding symptoms and beliefs. There have also been findings that demonstrate a positive association between compulsive buying and a poorly defined sense of identity (Claes, Müller & Luyckx, 2016).

The study carried out by Chou *et al.* (2018) was among the first to research the roles of self-criticism and shame in hoarding pathology, in particular hoarding beliefs and overall symptom severity. Their findings show that self-criticism and shame are positively associated with HD symptoms and hoarding-related beliefs.

CHAPTER 10

Community Impact

Generally speaking, people with lived experience of HD aren't motivated
to resolve clutter-related issues because they often don't concede the
extent of their clutter or associated problems. Combined with a lack of
insight, this can result in defensiveness and conflict with family, friends
and the wider community. Again, experience has taught me that people
who hoard usually won't deal with related problems until they have to –
when their back is against a wall and their options are limited.

Lack of insight about their condition and related risks and issues
is especially challenging if the person with HD also has a co-existing
condition such as bipolar disorder or schizophrenia, where anosognosia[1]
is a common symptom that impairs a person's ability to recognise their
own illness. Fear of stigma, judgement, shame and embarrassment also
leads people with HD to avoid the issue and they often become socially
isolated.

Excessive clutter can present a barrier to a person receiving vital
help and support at home. It can also affect interpersonal relationships,
employment and housing status. Hoarding requires a greater amount of
external intervention, including the removal of a child, elder or pet from
the home, and eviction or threat of eviction (Tolin *et al.*, 2008).

But before contemplating intervention, as well as understanding the
individual's circumstances, it's also important to consider any wider community impact such as public protection issues, especially in high-density
areas.

People with little or no knowledge or experience of HD often fail to
understand why the person with HD 'needs to keep all that crap' or 'can't
just get rid of stuff'. As humans, we are predisposed to kindness and the

---

1 'Anosognosia' is a medical term to describe when someone is unaware of their own
   mental health condition or can't perceive their condition accurately. From the Greek
   meaning 'to not know a disease'.

desire to help others but equally, 'we all fear what we do not understand' (Brown, 2010, p.87).

Often, by the time a person's clutter is impacting the wider community, the situation has reached crisis point and while some of the risks and issues can be frightening or unpleasant, try to bear in mind that the individual with lived experience of HD most likely has at least one other comorbid health-related condition, and that they've probably been living with extreme clutter for many years, so any imminent intervention will undoubtedly cause them significant distress.

A question I often get asked is when a hoarding situation should be 'reported'. My answer is always focused around harm and assessment and safeguarding: the health, safety and wellbeing of the individual with HD as well as any other dependent person (or animal/s) in the home, especially a child or elderly adult who may be adversely affected by the situation. If there are any concerns about fire safety, environmental or public health, building structure and maintenance, daily living activities (food and hygiene) or animals, these should be raised with the relevant local government agency, housing provider or animal welfare organisation. Maintaining a health and safety focus helps to avoid any personal bias.

Generally speaking, when family members or friends try to intervene, albeit with good intentions, usually both the person with HD and their loved ones become frustrated or angry and a breakdown in the relationship ensues. I think it works best if a relevant professional can provide practical help and therapeutic support, and for family or friends to assist at a later stage in the process – encouraging maintenance of newly formed behaviours and strategies.

Family dynamics

HD can create a significant burden on families since anyone living under the same roof as a person with hoarding behaviours will be exposed to the same problems and risks. They, too, are likely to suffer distress (sometimes significantly more so) due to the associated challenges of living in an extremely cluttered home. Loved ones also feel shame, embarrassment, hopelessness and frustration because the person with HD is ambivalent about the situation. Sadly, negative emotions often cause conflict between family members and can ultimately lead to them becoming estranged.

The effects of these challenges can have a lifetime impact on children, with the associated psychological distress lasting into adulthood. Recent research indicates that adult children of people who hoard have reported feelings of grief related to the loss of their relationship with their parent, as well as anger stemming from beliefs that their parent who hoards chose possessions over their children (Neziroglu, 2020). And as their parents age, adult children of people who hoard experience additional responsibilities as caregivers, with the level of burden experienced found to be comparable with or greater than that reported by family members of people with dementia (Drury *et al.*, 2014).

Family dynamics add another potentially challenging dimension to a practitioner's role, especially if family members are living in the same home as the client with HD. If that is the case, I would encourage them to work together to agree some boundaries within the home, for example agreeing which rooms, areas or spaces are shared and should remain relatively clutter-free. In cases where a family member has made the referral on behalf of someone who lives alone, I'm always clear that my client is the person I am working with – the person who occupies the home, regardless of who owns the home or who is paying for my time.

Multi-agency approach

HD is a difficult condition to treat and even among other severe mental disorders HD is unique in requiring multi-disciplinary skills and expertise to address both the behaviours and the symptoms. Factors including co-morbidity, level of insight, fire safety, environmental and public health issues all require involvement from multi-agency organisations. However, a combined effort to achieve successful intervention will be expensive and is likely to take several months.

In 1998, Fairfax County Government Department in Virginia created a Hoarding Task Force, the first of its kind in the United States (Fairfax County, 2023), in response to calls for emergency services to attend hoarded homes 'as a way to combine the many resources within county agencies to provide a coordinated response to residential hoarding when it threatened life, safety, and property, as well as preventing deaths due to hoarding'. In 2010, partly due to the success of the Task Force, Fairfax County combined its agencies to create a Department of Code Compliance (DCC), providing a multi-enforcement code response. Since DCC would include coordinated responses to hoarding, the task force was renamed in 2012 as the Hoarding Committee. Fairfax County (2023) say:

Significant staff resources and assets are required for even the most min-imal involvement in an incident and working together ensures a faster resolution to the dangers and dilemmas that [home] owner/occupants face. To provide an intervention that will benefit both the owner/occu-pant and the community, a compassionate, professional, and coordinated approach must be developed.

Hear, hear!

Since 1998, at least 75 other communities across the USA have formed hoarding task forces. In the UK, there are a handful of hoarding commit-tees that I am aware of but there are dozens of versions of multi-agency hoarding protocols created by local government agencies, many of which I would argue are either incorrect, inappropriate or insufficient in their approach. I am frustrated not only by the sheer waste of limited resources but also by the lack of any oversight of the procedures documented in these protocols. I have been campaigning for the development and imple-mentation of national guidelines on HD treatment and intervention since May 2014, when the Chief Fire Officers Association (CFOA), now the National Fire Chiefs Council (NFCC), launched the first UK Hoarding Awareness Week (Freeman, 2014). I believe *ICD-11* (World Health Organ-isation, 2018) coming into effect in January 2022 has created needful circumstances for such guidelines.

Having worked with multiple local authority departments over the past ten years, I have learned that funds can usually be found for services to 'clear out', 'deep clean', or even the perceived 'softer' approach of 'decluttering' a person's home. However, securing funds from the same departments to procure specialist services to provide recommended evidence-based treatment for HD is challenging to say the least. I was once asked by a journalist if I thought the government needed to find more money to help people with HD. My answer was and still is, no! The money is there, but government departments need to spend it differently.

The absence of government guidelines places a burden of responsi-bility on housing, health and social care professionals to make decisions about HD-related problems even when they have little or no knowledge of the complexities of the condition, or the impact on the person with HD. Often what happens is the person making decisions, for example, a social worker or housing officer, reverts to their own standards and judgements about 'normal' levels of clutter and types of belongings that are deemed 'acceptable' in a home, and signposts to services seeking a quick resolution to the problematic clutter. The immense pressure placed on our health and social care services exacerbates the need to solve the problem as quickly as possible and move on to the next 'case'. In actual fact, this approach only serves to worsen the problem for both the person trying to help and the person with HD, for whom it can be catastrophic or even fatal.

CHAPTER 11

Assessing Risks and Issues

To help remove subjectivity as well as provide a common language that can be adopted by multi-agency teams and multi-disciplinary professionals, making use of assessment tools supports prioritisation and decision-making about the types of intervention required. The Clutter Image Rating Scale (CIRS) is probably the most widely used tool, but it is extremely important to note that *volume of clutter is only one feature that should be considered when assessing risks and issues.*

Also, assessment tools can still potentially be prejudiced by the person carrying out the assessment. For example, professionals from different disciplines may focus on different elements of the questionnaire and their responses may be influenced by their knowledge and experience and how they interpret subjective words such as 'safe' and 'accessible'. With that in mind, I am excited to be able to share the following new Home Environment Assessment Tool for Hoarding (HEATH©), which I have been keenly awaiting since I contributed feedback during its development.

Home Environment Assessment Tool for Hoarding (HEATH©)

This tool was created by the Centre for Collaborative Research on Hoarding at the University of British Columbia (UBC) to assess the most important health and safety risks in hoarded environments. Risk assessment in hoarded homes is not easy. Different service providers often have different priorities when working in the home, as well as different understandings of what risk means. With this in mind, the UBC Centre collaborated with community partners such as fire inspectors, social workers and housing providers to create the HEATH©. This universal tool is designed for professionals in any discipline or area of community practice working with hoarding. It will enable service providers from diverse disciplines to communicate more effectively and plan hoarding interventions based on shared priorities.

A colour version of the HEATH©, as well as guidance and tips on using the tool, is available at: https://hoarding.psych.ubc.ca/knowledge-exchange/heath.

I wouldn't be surprised if HEATH© becomes the universally adopted 'go-to' tool that will over time supersede many of the earlier questionnaires. Having tools such as this is incredibly valuable, not only for the assessment and evaluation of risks and issues, but also for providing related professionals with a common language and shared understanding. I especially like HEATH© because it supports a harm-reduction attitude to extreme clutter and hoarding.

Other tools and questionnaires are listed below.

HOMES© (Health, Obstacles, Mental Health, Endangerment, Structure & Safety)

(Bratiotis *et al.*, 2011)

A multi-disciplinary risk assessment tool that provides a structural measure through which the level of risk in a severely cluttered environment can be conceptualised.

Home Environment Index

(Steketee & Frost, 2013, pp.221–2)

A 15-item questionnaire that can be completed by the client or related professional to quickly assess the home environment and identify and health and safety issues.

Activities of Daily Living for Hoarding (ADL-H)

(Steketee & Frost, 2013, p.219)

The ADL-H asks the client to select the option that best represents the degree of difficulty they experience in undertaking activities because of the clutter or hoarding problem.

Hoarding Interview

(Steketee & Frost, 2013, pp.208–13)

Ideally, this semi-structured interview would happen in the home to allow the interviewer to observe the physical space and gain an understanding of the causes and impact of the accumulated clutter. Conducting the interview in a conversational style manner will help to establish a good rapport between client and helper.

Clutter Image Rating Scale

(Steketee & Frost, 2013, p.217)

Useful to determine the severity of clutter in the home. It is one of the most widely used assessment tools, perhaps due to its simplicity since users can point to the image that most closely represents the amount of clutter in each room of the house.

Clutter – Hoarding Scale©

(Institute for Challenging Disorganization, 2011)

An assessment measurement tool, developed by the Institute for Challenging Disorganization® (ICD®) to give professional organisers and related professionals definitive parameters related to health and safety.

Saving Inventory – Revised

(Steketee & Frost, 2013, pp.215–16)

A 23-item questionnaire for completion by the client to assess acquiring and saving behaviours as well as impact on the home environment.

CHAPTER 12

Fire and Safety

In 2024, the Scottish Fire and Rescue Service, the UK's largest and the world's fourth largest fire brigade, reported that in the last five years 61 per cent of all accidental dwelling fire fatalities were people aged 60 and over, and more than a third of accidental dwelling fire casualties were also people aged 60 and over. Combined with the knowledge that the prevalence of clinically impairing HD in populations over age 55 is greater than 6 per cent, it brings the level of risk into sharp focus.

Hoarding has the potential to increase the risk of a fire developing and restrict the ability of householders to make a safe escape. In the event of a fire, a blocked or compromised escape route can lead to serious injury or even death. It also puts other people in neighbouring and adjoining properties at risk from the excessive smoke and quickly developing fire. Fires can also become hotter due to the number of flammable items stored within a property. Firefighters who respond to a fire can be put at risk, due to obstructions at the entrances or windows, falling objects and excessive quantities of stored materials that can lead to collapse. It can also be difficult to locate casualties within rooms that are severely cluttered.

Other impacts on the attending firefighters include difficulty in locating electrical, gas and other utility shut-offs. Getting water to the scene of any fire can also be made harder, and the amount of water used can make items unstable with the potential for toppling over. An overloaded structure such as a floor or wall can become weaker if water is absorbed by the excessive number of items, leading to collapse.

If you work with people who have lived experience of HD, it is important that you have fire safety awareness information that will allow you to assess the property and give practical advice and guidance to the people you are supporting.

Fire and rescue services offer free guidance on fire safety and some also offer home fire safety visits (or an equivalent). These visits offer free, personalised advice to householders and in some instances fire detection can be fitted during the visit. Industry tools such as the Clutter Image Rating Scale have been adopted by many fire services to assist firefighters to identify and assess levels of clutter and this information can be passed on when making a referral to any related professionals.

Allowing a member of the fire service into a property can be distressing for some people, and it is good practice to arrange a joint visit with someone they know and perhaps trust to help calm any nerves and provide support in applying any advice following the visit. As well as specialist practitioners, trusted people can include, carers, family members or related professionals. Information on how to make a referral for a home safety visit can be found on your local fire service website.

Some things to consider:

- Does the house have fire detection fitted? Is there working smoke and heat detection throughout and is it tested regularly? Is extra detection required due to severe clutter or in specific areas of the home, for example the bedroom, due to additional risks such as smoking?

- Are escape routes kept free from items? Can the front and/or back door be opened freely?

- Are hallways and staircases kept clear? If not, highlight the dangers to the householder of this and the impact it may have on anyone visiting the property or in escaping in the event of a fire (including firefighters). Keys to the property should be kept in the door or near at hand.

- Are there people who use medication in the property? This can be dangerous if medication makes the householder tired or drowsy, especially if smoking or cooking.

- Are there people who smoke in the property? Provide advice on the dangers of smoking in or near flammable items such as newspapers or clothing, and whether the householder can smoke outside or in the room with the least number of items. Advise never to smoke in bed. Care should be taken if flammable emollient creams are in use.

- Is medical home oxygen in use? The addition of concentrated oxygen into the room, or on to clothing and bedding, will greatly increase the intensity of a fire should one start. If someone in the home uses medial oxygen, adhere to the following advice:

- Never smoke (including e-cigarettes) or be near someone who smokes when using home oxygen.
- Never charge electronic devices (such as phones, tablets, laptops, e-cigarettes or games consoles) in rooms where oxygen is being used or stored.
- Smoke alarms should be fitted in the rooms where oxygen is used.
- Stay away from naked flames (e.g. lit matches, lighters).

- Are the cooker and kitchen worktops kept clear of flammable items such as tea towels or paper towels? If not, this poses a potential fire risk, as does cooking being done on a portable or camping stove.

- How is the home heated? Look out for the use of portable heaters. If the central heating/radiators, which can be particularly dangerous if they are placed on an unbalanced surface or items are placed too close to them.

- Are candles being used? Are proper holders in use and on hard, stable surfaces? Does the householder snuff out candles if leaving the property, or exiting the room before going to sleep? It may be evident that ceiling lights are not able to be used and surfaces for table lamps are not available. LED flameless candles are a safer option.

- Are electrical sockets overloaded? Are electrical sockets visible or are they hidden from view? Look out for the 'daisy chaining' of extension leads where one is plugged into another to give extra length, and the use of cable drums within the home.

- Switch off and unplug all electrical appliances not designed to be left on overnight as they could overheat and catch fire.

- Don't overcharge mobile phones or use when charging.

- The use of block adapters is not recommended because the weight of plugs can cause the adapter to become loose from the socket, and arcing – where electricity jumps from one connection to another –may result in the adaptor overheating and catching fire.

- Does the householder have a night-time routine?

  - Switch off and unplug all electrical appliances not designed to be left on overnight.
  - Stub out all cigarettes and always empty ashtrays. Pour water over cigarette ends and matches before putting them in the bin outside.
  - Put fireguards around open fires. Do not build up the fire before going to bed.
  - Switch off portable heaters.
  - Do not put on washing machines, tumble driers or dishwashers overnight.
  - Close all doors if it is possible to do so – it can keep escape routes free from smoke and may stop a fire spreading.
  - Make sure the main door keys are to hand.
  - Have a working phone beside the bed.

- Does the householder have a fire escape plan?

  Plan A

  - The first-choice route of escape is always through the main door. Make sure it is closed once everyone is out.

  Plan B

  - If it's not safe to leave by the main door, what other escape options are there? Is there another door that could be used, or a fire escape?
  - Is it possible to climb out of a ground floor window? Is it possible to climb out of a first-floor window onto a garage roof or extension and get down safely?

  If Plan A or B are not safe, it might be possible to find somewhere to stay safe and await rescue. Everything should be left ready so that the person can:

  - go to a room with a phone and a window that opens
  - pack clothes and blankets around the door to keep smoke out
  - stay by the window and shout for help.

CHAPTER 13

Environmental Health

I often say that when I first go to visit a client in their home I imagine having a firefighter on one shoulder and an environmental health officer on the other because my main concern is for their health and safety, and that of anyone else visiting the property. I have learned a lot from skilled and experienced professionals in those fields.

Many moons ago, I was invited by Pat Hoey to speak at an event hosted by the Royal Environmental Health Institute of Scotland (REHIS). Although now retired, Pat is a Fellow of REHIS (an award presented in recognition of outstanding and distinguished service to the work of the Institute) and someone I now have the pleasure of calling my friend. Pat took time out of his busy retirement schedule to pen some words that provide an environmental health perspective on hoarding:

> Environmental health officers often come into contact with people who have lived experience of hoarding and occasionally may be the first professional to do so. It has always been challenging and not always dealt with in the most sensitive manner. Previously, it was considered a 'lifestyle choice' by many individuals who now understand it to be a mental health condition. Often the first contact comes via a complaint from a neighbour regarding odour entering their home from an adjoining property, or perhaps seeing excessive numbers of insects at the window. Referrals also come from social landlords, fire safety officers and social workers, concerned for the safety of the individual and seeking advice on the health risks to the occupier and how to resolve the issues raising concern. Many of the issues will be obvious, others not so.
>
> - **Odour:** Perhaps the prevalent complaint from others and usually indicates that the hoarding behaviour is problematic. Neighbours who can smell the odour inside their own home from next door can often have their quality of life reduced, and their mental health challenged because they have no control nor remedy other than

involvement of outside agencies. Within the home of the person with HD there are likely to be issues with putrescible material such as body fluids, human or animal faeces or food waste. These in turn can cause other problems with health implications. Odour in itself is not likely to cause infection or disease but can certainly lead to feelings of nausea for visitors to the home.

- **Pests:** Where there are deposits of animal, human or food waste they are likely to encourage the breeding of insects or rodents. Rats and mice are known to spread disease, so their presence should not be tolerated. They can also spread to adjoining properties. Where there is an indication that there is a problem, it is imperative to contact Environmental Health for assistance. Some insects do have implications for disease carrying while others would be considered more of a nuisance. Cockroaches are considered a health risk as they can spread bacteria and may also infest adjoining properties. Biting insects such as fleas may be difficult to treat in a person with HD's home, particularly if the source is a pet and the home is extremely cluttered. Their presence can also be problematic for visitors to the home. Bedbugs are not known to spread disease but their presence, often in large numbers, can affect the mental health of those constantly bitten. They can also spread between properties and need expert treatment for elimination. Other insects, such as fruit flies, do not cause disease and are non-biting, but would be considered a nuisance as they can be found in large numbers within unsanitary homes. In general, where pests are likely to be present, Environmental Health should be consulted to assess the situation and can assist in identifying the pests and formulating a plan for their control.

- **Dampness:** People with lived experience of HD and/or Diogenes syndrome may reach a stage where they not only stop looking after themselves but neglect the maintenance of their property. This can lead to dampness within the home, for example from plumbing leaks or lack of roof maintenance. It is fundamental to good health that we live in dry homes so as part of the recovery plan, the source of any water leaks should be eradicated. Also, there may be issues with condensation dampness, particularly in homes that are poorly heated and ventilated, and have poor insulation. This often leads to mould formation on surfaces, even on stored clothing. Moulds can cause allergic reactions, such as sneezing and runny nose, and can irritate the eyes and cause skin rashes. It can be particularly problematic for asthma sufferers. Again, Environmental Health can assist in identifying causes of dampness and assist in a plan to remedy these matters.

- **Accumulations:** There can be a risk of physical injury due to the volume and placement of items. Even if there is no issue with the type of items stored, such as clothing or newspapers, there is a risk of falling or the items toppling onto the occupier (or visitor). In addition, the volume and weight of items may overload the structure-bearing beams of the property with a danger of collapse. This is obviously a major concern within flatted dwellings and the risks to occupiers below. It may be worthy of a call to Building Control if there are concerns of this nature, who will be able to advise. Where there is no clear route to utilities such as those in bathrooms and kitchens there would be a general health concern. How does the occupier access and use a toilet if there is no clear route in and out? How is food prepared and stored if there is no access to the kitchen? Similarly, is there safe access to a sleeping area? The absence of their availability would have a detrimental effect on the occupier's quality of life and should be dealt with as quickly as can be allowed.

Environmental health officers have broad ranging powers which are mainly used when the activities and behaviour of an individual cause 'nuisance' to others. They must serve notice in accordance with their local government legislation where nuisance is identified and can request works to be carried out to abate the nuisance. Where the works are not carried out by the date specified, they can arrange for the works to be done and claim back costs from the 'author of the nuisance', which would generally be the person living in the home in these cases. It is a blunt instrument where the person is not affecting others beyond their own self-neglect, and the carrying out of works may be detrimental to their mental health. There will be occasions where works must be carried out, for instance if plumbing leaks affect a downstairs neighbour's property, but the rush to clear houses should be avoided without careful consideration of the person's situation and needs.

Having now examined the cognitive behavioural model for understanding hoarding and the many tools and professional guidance available, in the next part we deliberate the recommended evidence-based therapeutic treatments that can be applied to help those with lived experience of HD.

Part Three

SEEK A THERAPEUTIC APPROACH

LEARNING OBJECTIVE

Following deliberation of therapies, approaches and attitudes in relation to HD, it is expected that the reader will be able to develop an action plan that is appropriate for the client and their situation.

CHAPTER 14

Clearouts

Few people with HD/CD/ND receive any type of help or support and usually for those who do experience an intervention it is in response to fire and safety concerns, a risk of homelessness, or an inability to receive care at home services. And while I believe the mental health classification of HD has gone some way to improving our understanding of this mental disorder, what is needed more urgently are accessible therapeutic treatment pathways for those seeking and in need of help and support.

Encouragingly, in the last couple of years or so, I have seen an increase in the number of people with HD and/or CD/ND reaching out themselves to ask for help, but the majority are still living with this 'hidden disorder' because they feel embarrassed or ashamed, they fear stigma and judgement, or feel anxious about the potential outcomes, specifically a clearout of their home and the loss of their belongings.

Once upon a time, some people thought hoarding was a quick and easy problem to solve; by securing the services of a house clearance company the issue would be dealt with in a matter of days. However, studies (Kysow *et al.*, 2020) and experience tell us enforced clearouts are both traumatic and ineffective, and without any behavioural therapy almost 100 per cent of people will revert to hoarding behaviours, but do so more rapidly due to heightened levels of stress and anxiety. Hence, the reality is that clearouts create more problems by only addressing the symptom rather than the cause of the disorder. Even the threat of a clearout can be damaging as it's likely to raise fears, create mistrust and cause relationships to deteriorate.

Clearouts, especially if enforced, cause significant distress, leaving the person with feelings of despair and hopelessness that sometimes result in them being hospitalised following a suicide attempt or tragically dying by suicide. Bratiotis *et al.* (2011, p.19) share the experience of a health inspector who, following clearouts, said:

> In all three instances of going in and cleaning these places up, within weeks of relocating the individual back into a clean environment, the individual passed away...it was such a dramatic change for them...we didn't realize the impact of the sociological change.

Prior to the release of *DSM-5* in 2013 and *ICD-11* in 2018, with the inclusion of HD as a distinct mental disorder, enforced clearouts could perhaps be more easily defended in the absence of clinical guidance. Today, this is indefensible. I believe it is fundamentally wrong to consider enforced clearouts as an acceptable intervention for HD. Enforced clearouts are a misuse of what is quite often public funds, and a violation of an individual's human rights under the Human Rights Act 1998, specifically the 'right to respect for private and family life' and 'protection of property', where everyone is entitled to the peaceful enjoyment of their possessions.

I fully appreciate that there will be situations when the clearout of a person's home is necessary, but I implore you to consider this as an exception and only when all other approaches have been exhausted, and the clearance of items should be proportionate to the scale of the problem. For example, when there is an endangerment risk to public health and safety, a breach of a housing tenancy agreement leading to the property falling into disrepair, or an adult safeguarding issue, only those areas presenting risk should be cleared, and not the entire contents of the home. I also believe that, in line with adult safeguarding legislation, every attempt should be made to include the person with HD as much as possible in the planning stages of a clearout. By way of an example, let's consider the principles underlying the Adult Support and Protection (Scotland) Act 2007; I'm confident that your local government body will have something very similar:

Principles underlying the Act

The overarching principle underlying Part 1 of the Act is that any intervention in an individual's affairs should provide **benefit** to the individual and should be the **least restrictive** option of those that are available which will meet the purpose of the intervention. This is supported by a set of guiding principles which, together with the overarching principle, must be taken account of when performing functions under Part 1 of the Act. These are:

- the wishes and feelings of the adult at risk (past and present).

- the views of other significant individuals, such as the adult's nearest relative; their primary carer, guardian, or attorney; or any other person with an interest in the adult's wellbeing or property.

- the importance of the adult taking an active part in the performance of the function under the Act.

- providing the adult with the relevant information and support to enable them to participate as fully as possible.

- the importance of ensuring that the adult is not treated less favourably than another adult in a comparable situation; and

- the adult's abilities, background, and characteristics (including their age, sex, sexual orientation, religious persuasion, racial origin, ethnic group and cultural and linguistic heritage). (Scottish Government, 2022)

Having shared my somewhat polemic views on clearouts, let's move on to discussing more positive interventions.

CHAPTER 15

Therapeutic Treatments

Helping people affected by HD requires a great deal of patience and compassion. I was disheartened to recently read that:

> seemingly, clinicians report more frustration with hoarding clients than with non-hoarding ones. They are more often irritated by the client's behaviour and relieved when the client misses a session and have frequent feelings of wanting the client to transfer to another therapist. (Rodriguez & Frost, 2023, p.12)

Reading this reminded me of an encounter I had with a clinical psychologist not long after setting up Life-Pod. I had approached them to discuss a collaborative therapy approach but when they said: 'As a therapist, your heart sinks when someone with OCD walks into your clinic,' I walked away feeling sad and really quite angry. I was tempted to go back and ask them how they think the people who showed courage by asking for their help would feel hearing them making statements like that. Instead, I resolved that my 'can do' attitude would empower me to support people in any way I could, to be a giver of help and hope!

But I am curious as to why those clinicians might become irritated and experience these feelings of wanting the client to transfer to another therapist. I read with interest a paper written by Green, Carrillo and Betancourt (2002) titled 'Why the disease-based model of medicine fails our patients' that states, 'Whereas disease defines a pathophysiologic process, illness is defined by the complete person – physical, psychological, social, and cultural (Eisenberg, 1977)' (p.142). The paper discusses how our individual experience of being unwell is a unique representation of our illness, and asking some pertinent questions during a conversation with clients will help to uncover any cultural or social norms, allowing treatment for the client and not just their disease. However, the paper goes on to question whether physicians will in reality be able to adopt this conversational approach and concludes by saying 'the healing tools and instruments of science are blunt and ineffective when used blindly in ignorance of the meaning and context of a person's illness. We need to foster attitudes, values, and communication skills that focus on illness, not just disease' (p.143).

> Medicine is both the art and science of healing. The science is clearly manifest in all medical school curricula and graduate medical training. The art, however, is subtle and receives far less emphasis. It is character-ized, in part, by the ability to apply the science of medicine to individual patients' unique illness, with particular attention to the nuances of social circumstance and culture. (Green *et al.*, 2002, p.142)

Unfortunately, many physicians are still ignorant about HD; in part I think because it is newly classified and not helped by the fact that presently there are no NICE (National Institute for Health and Care), SIGN (Scot-tish Intercollegiate Guidelines Network) or other similar international clinical guidelines for hoarding that would help them to ask pertinent questions and have a conversation that could lead to them providing consistent, evidence-based practice for people with lived experience of the disorder. Combined with the knowledge that people with HD tend not to talk about the condition and are unlikely to proactively broach the subject with their physician, it becomes more apparent why clients often don't receive an intervention until they reach a point of crisis. In an attempt to help both clients and physicians, and inspired by Rudge's (2018) ice-breaker form, I created a more streamlined version named *HD Conversation Starter* (Fay, 2024) as a resource that can be used to prompt and guide a discussion about hoarding and getting help or support.

Treatment for HD generally requires a greater number of treatment sessions than other psychiatric disorders (Wootton *et al.*, 2019). Remem-bering that around half of people who hoard are genetically predisposed to the condition, and the other half have experienced trauma, it is truly humbling when they allow you into their home and share their story with you. It's a popular misconception that people with HD are happy with their home environment. Mostly, they are overwhelmed, and have feelings of hopelessness and despair. Often, they want things to be different, but they don't know what to do or how to go about it. But always, always they want to be treated with respect and listened to without judgement by someone they can trust who will see them, and not just their clutter.

I believe the optimum intervention for hoarding is a combination of cognitive and behavioural therapies, including motivational interviewing techniques and personal coaching methods to instil confidence and cultivate abilities to plan, organise and develop. These skills, combined with a harm-reduction attitude and an overall aim of improving a person's health, safety and wellbeing by reducing their acquiring and saving behaviours, can be carried out successfully by a trained specialist practitioner with the client in their home.

At the time of writing, my team of 14 practitioners at Life-Pod are supporting around 90 clients in their homes, ranging from two to six hours per week. Every client and their situation is unique and not one of them has received a formal diagnosis of HD. We have no pre-prescribed way of doing things; our practice is completely client-centred and we adopt a pragmatic, therapeutic approach with a harm-reduction attitude – working at the client's pace to achieve long-term success. Our primary aim is to make a client safer and more secure in their home, and our objective is two-fold: (1) to help a client understand their reasons for acquiring and saving belongings, and (2) to help a client develop skills that will enable them to better organise or let go of some of their belongings. Our practice incorporates coaching and motivation techniques to inspire behaviour change as well as advocating on behalf of the people we work with.

CHAPTER 16

Understanding Depression and Anxiety

As we know, HD frequently co-occurs with depression and anxiety – 92 per cent of those with HD have received at least one additional mental health diagnosis, including anxiety disorders and depression (Frost & Hristova, 2011), with the majority being major depressive disorders (Archer *et al.*, 2019). I therefore believe it is important for us to understand as much as possible about these conditions so we can apply therapeutic techniques more effectively and in a more considered way.

As well as my own lived experience of both depression and anxiety, prior to setting up Life-Pod, I volunteered with Action on Depression, a Scottish charity which sadly no longer exists. My role involved delivering online coaching for individuals who wanted to learn CBT-based skills to help them manage difficulties they were experiencing with depression, low mood or anxiety.

I have learned how to 'manage' my depressive episodes, but I am acutely aware of just how debilitating this condition can be. Depression is a distressing experience that affects how a person feels physically and mentally. It creates an 'extreme sadness that shrouds a person's perception of everyday life; causes periods of anger, sadness, loneliness, hatred, and anxiety that [disables] the mind from making even the simplest of decisions. Choices become painful and overwhelming, and seclusion becomes necessary' (Nurses With Heart, 2023).

Factors that contribute to depression can be complex and may vary widely between clients, but some common symptoms (NHS Inform, 2023) that could impact you working together include:

- **psychological symptoms** – low mood, feeling hopeless and helpless, low self-esteem, tearful, irritable, low tolerance, lacking motivation, difficulty making decisions, and self-harming or having suicidal thoughts

- **physical symptoms** – moving or speaking more slowly than usual, aches and pains, lacking energy, or tiredness due to disrupted sleep patterns

- **social symptoms** – avoiding contact and missing or cancelling sessions.

In layman's terms, anxiety is typically described as a feeling of apprehension or fear, usually relating to perceived rather than actual threat, and our automatic physiological reaction to the situation is what's known as the 'fight or flight' response, where our body reacts by releasing adrenaline into our system. This results in symptoms including increased heart rate or palpitations, chest pain, breathlessness, increased sweating or sweaty palms, dizziness, tingling sensations, feeling shaky, weakness or trembling and headaches. Again, these are things to be mindful of that may impact your work with the client. Specific strategies you can implement, such as grounding techniques, are included in Chapter 31.

CHAPTER 17

Cognitive Behavioural Therapy

Developed in the 1960s by psychiatrist Aaron Beck (1921–2021), cognitive behavioural therapy (CBT) isn't one single therapy but a group of techniques that can be used for a wide variety of mental health conditions, and is based on the concept that how we think about something can affect how we feel about it and how we behave as a consequence.

Therapeutic approaches that could help people with HD/CD/ND include:

- **cognitive therapy** to recognise distortions in thinking that are creating problems

- **behaviour therapy** to examine and change problematic thoughts based on reality

- **problem-solving therapy** to identify the problem, propose different solutions and implement only one of them

- **motivational interviewing** to examine problematic behaviour using a guiding style of communication to inspire change

- **mindfulness** to focus on the present moment without judgement or reaction to thoughts and feelings

- **acceptance and commitment therapy** to accept unpleasant thoughts and feelings.

You can see some of these approaches incorporated into the Model for Understanding HD (Frost & Hartl, 1996; Steketee & Frost, 2003), where cognitive restructuring (also known as 'thinking errors' or 'cognitive distortions'), sometimes referred to as a 'mental filter', is used to help people with HD to identify unhelpful thoughts and irrational beliefs about their belongings as well as how their emotions affect their acquiring and saving behaviours.

Cognitive distortions are associated with all types of mental health problems (Beck et al., 1979; Clark & Beck, 2010); below are some of the most common thinking errors.

All-or-nothing

Black and white thinking that doesn't allow for shades of grey. Often accompanies perfectionistic standards; exemplified by use of words like most, everything, and nothing.

> 'This is the most beautiful teapot I've ever seen; I'll never see another one like it and if I don't buy it now I'll have missed a great opportunity to own it.'

Over-generalisation

Viewing a single negative event as a pattern that will happen over and over again; exemplified by use of words like 'always' and 'never'.

> 'Every time I get rid of something, I always discover I need it later so I'm not getting rid of anything ever again.'

Jumping to conclusions

Negative interpretation of events without facts to support beliefs; predicting that things will turn out badly.

> 'I know all my friends think I'm lazy and just can't be bothered to tidy up; they think I'm being rude and selfish when I don't invite them into my home.'

Catastrophising

Exaggerating the importance of an item and minimising capabilities for obtaining needed information.

> 'If I put this away and can't remember where it is right when I need it, I'll be disastrous.'

Discounting the positive

Thinking that positive experiences don't count.

> 'I got the kitchen cleared and I can now cook again, but it makes no difference because every other room is still full of stuff I need to sort through.'

Emotional reasoning

Allowing emotions to determine logical reasoning and confusing facts with feelings.

> 'The sales assistant went through to the back to get this specially for me; it's not exactly what I wanted and it's the wrong size, but I bought it anyway because I don't want to disappoint them.'

Moral reasoning

Applying unwritten rules or expectations you feel you should live up to. This is an emotional or behavioural response to situations that you believe can never be changed. Also associated with perfectionistic standards and illustrated by use of words like 'must' and 'should'.

> 'I must call the doctor tomorrow; I ought to have done it weeks ago, but I shouldn't feel like this. It's not fair.'

Labelling

Attaching a negative label to oneself or others; similar to an extreme form of all-or-nothing thinking.

> 'I've tried everything to get myself organised, but nothing works; I'm such a failure.'

Underestimating oneself

Underrating personal ability to cope with adversity and stress.

> 'If I don't get this, I'll be utterly devastated and won't be able to handle it.'

Overestimating oneself

Assuming greater capability to accomplish a task than is reasonable to expect.

'I've taken a couple of days off work to sort out my whole house.'

CBT is recognised as the recommended treatment for HD, but studies found that the number of patients demonstrating clinically significant change was low, ranging from 25 per cent to 43 per cent (Tolin *et al.*, 2015), indicating that CBT isn't a wholly effective treatment intervention for reducing symptoms of hoarding behaviour.

Group CBT treatment has the advantage of improving the efficiency of treatment, and studies suggest that the group format also helps to improve motivation and treatment adherence due to increased peer support (Muroff *et al.*, 2009). However, preliminary research has demonstrated that individuals with HD prefer individual treatment over group-based treatments (Robertson, Paparo & Wootton, 2020).

CHAPTER 18

Innovative Technology-Based Interventions

In 2015, I worked with a team of graduate students at Napier University in Edinburgh to develop the Life-Pod app based on CBT techniques. The app allows a user to set goals and establish the following strategies to help reduce acquiring and saving behaviours:

- Rules (to help decision-making about compulsive acquisitions).

- Rerouting (to identify plans and ideas for alternative activities).

- Ruminating (to consider the advantages and disadvantages of an acquisition).

- Rewards (to recognise and celebrate achievement of goals).

The app also includes a journal and tracker that can be shared via email with a therapist or practitioner, for example. Unfortunately, technology develops very quickly these days, and the app needs some improvements and modifications. I am currently exploring the latest design and technology options for its redevelopment.

Still, it's pleasing to see new and emerging innovative technology-based treatments for HD, such as web-based software and virtual reality (VR). Currently, there is limited research, but VR has been effective in the treatment of related disorders such as social phobia, OCD, and generalised anxiety disorder (St-Pierre-Delorme & O'Connor, 2016). VR could be used in conjunction with home visits, or even as an alternative to home visits if for whatever reason access to a client's home isn't an option at that time. One study that used VR to simulate participants' home environments without existing clutter found that participants reported higher confidence and motivation to engage in behaviour change post immersion (Chasson *et al.*, 2020).

The Covid-19 pandemic forced all of us to embrace web-based technology, which for some has since become their new 'normal' as they continue using technology routinely to carry out daily activities, including meetings, minor medical assessments, training and so on. At Life-Pod, during Covid-19 restrictions, we trialled providing help and support for our clients by phone or using web-based software such as Zoom and Teams. While this method restricted some of the hands-on practical activities we could carry out, it proved to be a beneficial way to keep in touch with clients, especially those who had little or no contact with anyone else. We were able to set 'homework', such as a sorting exercise, and then arrange an agreed date and time for collection of any unwanted items to be discarded. Using the phone or web-based technology allowed us to continue to coach and motivate clients to achieve their goals and discuss any challenges they faced while working on their own to complete specific tasks and activities. Today, we incorporate technology into our practice to provide a blended support service where this is necessary and beneficial.

CHAPTER 19

Engagement, Change and Motivation

Client engagement

As mentioned in the Preface, even before creating Life-Pod my professional practice was focused on change and engagement for which there are several methodologies, but the one key element they all share that will strongly influence success or failure of the process is you, and more specifically, your interpersonal style. Research shows that a practitioner's belief in a client's ability to change has a strong impact on outcomes.

'They won't engage' is a statement I often hear from people. My response is always the same; I ask, 'What do you mean by that?' which usually gets a response of something along the lines of 'They won't let me in to help them get rid of stuff.' If, when trying to engage and motivate another person you tend to use phrases like 'You should...' or 'You must...' – described by psychoanalyst Albert Ellis as 'musturbation' – you are likely to elicit feelings of frustration and receive a defensive response. Similarly, when making statements such as 'I should do this' or 'I must do that' in relation to ourselves, we are likely to create feelings of shame, guilt and even self-loathing.

Instead, try thinking about what you are aiming to achieve and turn it into a question. For example, if your aim is to encourage the person to remove the refuse from the home, you could ask, 'Are you able to manage sorting the rubbish and recycling on your own?', 'Could I help you to gather some items from that room and put them in the recycling bin on my way out?' or 'How would you feel if I organised an uplift for those bulky items you no longer need or want?' Asking questions in this way will make the person feel that they have a choice and allows them (and you) to have a different perspective.

When we're asking someone to make a behaviour change, to achieve success we need to fully engage them in the process and affect sustainable change at a manageable pace. This again underpins why enforced clea-routs don't work and create 'future shock', a term coined by Alvin Toffler in his book (1970) of the same name to describe too much change in too short a period of time. Toffler hypothesised that we each have a threshold for dealing with change and when this is surpassed it triggers stress and disorientation. I believe that if we adopt the right mind-set and approach to helping people with lived experience of HD or CD we can counteract 'shock' with solace.

Our 'mind-set', shaped by our beliefs, how we think and how we feel, has a symbiotic relationship with how we act (our behaviour). Potentially, there may be an opportunity to shift a person's mindset while engaging them in conversation, and according to Daryl Conner, an international change 'guru', there are two key elements of a person's mindset that we should focus on if we're attempting to create a shift: (1) frame of refer-ence, and (2) priorities. Each of us has a unique frame of reference based on factors such as familial and professional backgrounds, experiences, education and so on, that inform our attitudes and assumptions. CBT and motivational interviewing (MI) can help to shift mindsets and reframe unhelpful thoughts and beliefs. The UK National Health Service adopts a technique called 'catch it, check it, change it', which suggests stepping back and challenging unhelpful thoughts by thinking about what evidence exists to support them, with the aim that over time these can be changed into helpful thoughts and behaviours.

Cycle of change

If you've ever tried to change a habit, you'll know it doesn't happen over-night. According to a study 'How are habits formed' (Lally, 2010), on average, it takes 66 days for a new habit to form. Habits involve a direct cue-behaviour association in memory. When encountered, cues activate a single, specific well-learned behavioural response. Habits are acquired as a consequence of a history of cue-contingent behavioral repetition. Evidence shows that established habits are cue-contingent, share features of automaticity, and are goal- or reward-independent (Hagger *et al.*, 2020).

According to researchers James Prochaska and Carlo DiClemente (1982), we move through six different stages when attempting to change our behaviour. These stages, as illustrated in Figure 19.1: The Transtheo-retical Model (Stages of Change), are pre-contemplation, contemplation, preparation, action, maintenance and termination (or relapse). Each stage requires us to adopt different strategies to move us to the next stage. The model, which evolved through studies relating to smoking cessation and comparisons between people who accessed treatment to help them to stop smoking and people who were able to stop smoking autonomously, operates on the assumption that people do not change behaviours quickly and do so only once they are ready. Change in behaviour, especially habitual behaviour, occurs continuously through a cyclical process (LaMorte, 2022), hence why it's sometimes referred to as the 'cycle of change'.

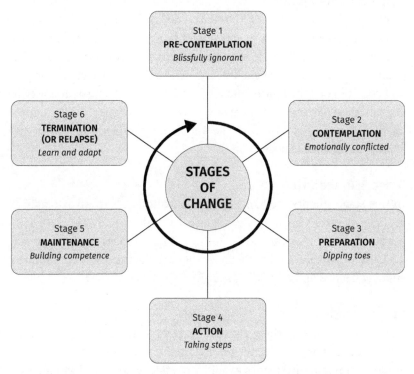

FIGURE 19.1: THE TRANSTHEORETICAL MODEL (STAGES OF CHANGE)

I want to re-emphasise the point made by LaMorte (2022) that The Transtheoretical Model operates on the assumption that people do not change behaviours quickly and decisively because, in my experience, people with HD are often ambivalent at best (or pre-contemplative) about the need or desire to change their hoarding-related behaviours, but when either a related professional, loved one, or member of the community becomes aware of the cluttered home they want to take action immediately. What we ought to consider is how best to help motivate the person to move through each of the cyclical stages using change strategies, as detailed below.

Stage 1: Pre-contemplation

In this stage, clients are unlikely to recognise or acknowledge any potential consequences resulting from excessive clutter-related problems, including threat of eviction or other intervention. We should accept rather than oppose this situation and adopt strategies that include asking the client to rethink their behaviour by analysing the risks of the status quo and considering potential benefits of making changes.

Stage 2: Contemplation

Clients recognise that their clutter is causing problems, but they have conflicted thoughts about the need to change their behaviour and often lack confidence in their ability to create change, which leads to a state of ambivalence. Strategies include asking the client to weigh up the pros and cons of both the status quo and making some changes. Identifying any potential barriers to change or discussing the client's ability to make changes may present you with the opportunity to instil hope that with some help, change is possible.

Stage 3: Preparation

In this stage, clients are likely to show a willingness towards making a change; even the smallest of changes is an indication of a client's commitment to move forward. Strategic tasks should focus on setting small, achievable goals and a plan to achieve them, including resources required, support needed and rewarding success.

Stage 4: Action

Clients begin putting their plan into action, demonstrating their commitment to making some changes. Each achievement will help to build a client's confidence in their own ability to effect change and will increase their motivation to keep going. Strategies focus on reviewing progress made and recognising success. Another strategic activity could involve discussing any help or support the client may need going forward to maintain the changes they have made.

Stage 5: Maintenance

This stage is entered into once the new habit is formed, which could take several months – remember that Lally's study (2010) revealed it can take up to 254 days before new behaviours become entrenched. Strategies should be focused on developing skills to cope with potential pitfalls, rerouting activities to avoid temptation, and creating the mindset that relapse is an expected part of the cycle and should be seen as a minor setback, not a complete failure.

Stage 6: Termination (or Relapse)

This stage reminds us that behaviour change can be difficult and sometimes a client may revert back to old habits if they feel as if the effort of maintaining the change outweighs the benefits gained by making the change. But change requires resistance and strategies should include helping the client to identify triggers and how to avoid these in the future. Some people may cycle through these stages of change several times before the behaviour becomes entrenched.

Although The Transtheoretical Model (TTM) can help to cultivate behavioural changes, critics (Adams & White, 2004) have highlighted some limitations in that it assumes the client has the capability to think rationally, make logical decisions and implement actions. They also argue that the validity of the TTM has not been established for complex health behaviours. 'Nevertheless, stage-targeted activity promotion interventions are more likely to induce changes in motivation as well as short-term behaviour changes' (Brug, 2004, p.247).

Motivating for change

Thanks to William Miller and Stephen Rollnick (2013), co-founders of motivational interviewing (MI), we have an evidence-based 'style' that was developed specifically to help people resolve ambivalence and strengthen their motivation for change. Miller and Rollnick point out that MI is not a 'technique', nor an 'easily learned gimmick' but a 'way of being with people'. First introduced in 1983 by Miller, recent meta-analyses show that MI is equivalent to or better than other treatments such as CBT (Hall, 2012).

> MI is a collaborative partnership with clients, a respectful evoking of their own motivation and wisdom, and a radical acceptance recognising that ultimately whether change happens is each person's own choice, an autonomy that cannot be taken away no matter how much one might wish to at times. (Hall, 2012, p.661)

The Transtheoretical Model discussed above has played a key role in the development of MI strategies that are designed to be used in in a non-threatening and supportive way to encourage a client to take responsibility for their own situation – examining their own circumstances, weighing up the pros and cons of changing, and making decisions about change. The first stage of change, *Pre-contemplation*, is often the most challenging and 'resistance to change is best summarised as the four R's: reluctance, rebellion, resignation, and rationalization' (DiClemente & Velasquez, 2002, p.204). Our role as practitioners is to determine why our client may be resistant to change and utilise MI strategies to positively diffuse resistance.

- **Reluctant** pre-contemplators are often unaware of the impact of their problematic behaviour and are generally more passively reluctant as opposed to being actively resistant to change. They may fear change, or don't want to disrupt the 'comfort zone' they have gotten used to. It will take time, empathy, and good communication to motivate these clients, specifically active listening skills.

- **Rebellious** pre-contemplators are usually fairly insightful about their problematic behaviour and won't appreciate being told what to do; they want to make their own decisions. They may appear unfriendly and resistant to change but this is perhaps driven by fear and insecurity. Allowing these clients to express their thoughts and feelings is important as well as trying to harness their energy in a positive way.

- **Resigned** pre-contemplators often lack energy and enthusiasm for change and can seem resigned to the situation or are overwhelmed by the problems created by their behaviour. They are likely to have made failed attempts to change and therefore may lack confidence in their own ability to effect change. These clients need to hear messages of hope and help to identify potential barriers, signalling that it's never too late to try again. Build their confidence one brick at a time and acknowledge success of each and every one.

- **Rationalising** pre-contemplators are generally not considering change because they tend to believe that their behaviour is the result of someone else's problem and not theirs. They will want to discuss at length their thoughts and rationale with the aim of strengthening their point of view. Again, empathy and communication skills, especially reflective listening, will be key to working well with these clients. Also, using strategies like decisional balance and asking these clients to consider the pros and cons of a situation are likely to be advantageous.

In 2013, Miller and Rollnick published their third edition of *Motivational Interviewing: Helping People Change*, which they state, 'is as different from the second [edition] (2002) as the second was from the first' edition, and 'more than 90 per cent of the writing is new' (2013, p.vii). I would highly recommend this book as a valuable and useful resource in your practice toolkit. Progressing from 'phases' and 'principles', the third edition introduces a four-process model consisting of engaging, focusing, evoking and planning but what has not, and must not, change is the 'spirit' of MI which is considered to be 'essential to good practice' and described as 'the mind-set and heart-set with which [MI] is practiced' (p.viii).

The 'spirit' is underpinned by the 'four processes' (Miller and Rollnick, 2013, pp.25-30), which, when applied, enhance our practice. Engaging is the first stage in the process where we aim to establish a helpful connection and a working relationship and is a prerequisite for everything that follows. Focusing is the process by which you develop and maintain a specific direction in the conversation about change. Then follows evoking, the part of the process that has always been at the core of MI and involves eliciting the client's own motivations for change. Planning encompasses both developing commitments to change and formulating a plan of action.

The four processes form what is termed the 'flow of MI'. They are both sequential and recursive; one does not stop as the next begins – they flow into each other, overlap, and recur. Below are some questions you can ask yourself during each process:

- Engaging (establishing a helpful connection and working relationship)

  - How comfortable is the client feeling while talking to me?
  - Am I being supportive and helpful?
  - Do I understand the situation from the client's perspective?

- Focusing (developing and maintaining a specific direction in the conversation about change)

  - Does the client have clear goals for making change?
  - Do I know what direction the client wants to go in?
  - Does this feel more like 'dancing' or 'wrestling'?

- Evoking (eliciting the client's own motivation for change)
  - What are the client's own reasons for change?
  - Does the client feel confident in their ability to change?
  - Am I moving too fast or going off track?

- Planning (developing commitment to change and formulating a concrete plan of action)
  - What would be a good first step toward change?
  - How can I help the client to move forward?
  - Did I ask permission before offering advice or necessary information?

Communications skills used throughout the four processes are: asking open-ended questions, affirming, reflective listening and summarising – referred to by the acronym OARS. The key to all of these skills is *active* listening (Gordon, 1970) and is a prerequisite to good MI practice. Used strategically, OARS and active listening can help people to move in the direction of change.

Open-ended questions invite the client to provide a more elaborate response and give you the opportunity to learn more about them.

Example: 'I understand you are concerned about what might happen to your belongings. Can you tell me more about that?'

Vs: 'Are you concerned about your belongings?'

Affirming statements show your understanding of the situation and help to build rapport with the client.

'I appreciate that this situation is really difficult for you. No wonder you feel overwhelmed, but you do seem to be quite resourceful since you've managed to cope with these challenges for the past few years.'

Reflective listening deepens your understanding of what the client expresses by rephrasing a statement in a way that explores the implicit meaning and feeling of the client's statement.

'It sounds as if you want to have all of your belongings out because it makes you feel better when you can see everything, and you don't want to forget what you have or where you put something. But you're worried about the impact and possibility of being evicted from your home. Before you saw your housing officer you weren't worried about it at all, but now you're really worried because they're saying that your stuff is a serious fire risk.'

Summarising links the discussion threads to ensure a mutual understanding of the situation and demonstrates that you listened and understood the client's perspective.

'Can I check with you that I've understood what we've discussed so far?

You prefer to keep your belongings out where you can see them but you're now worried that you might get evicted if you don't organise and get rid of some stuff because your housing officer says they're creating a fire safety issue? Does that sound about right?'

Conversely, it's also worth considering the '12 roadblocks' to good communication developed by Thomas Gordon (1970), a student and mentee of Carl Rogers whom he described as 'the most famous and respected psychologist in the world'. Gordon's 'roadblocks' (Gordon Training International, n.d.) are:

1. Ordering, directing, commanding

   'You have to...', 'You must...', 'You will...'

2. Warning, admonishing, threatening

   'If you don't, then...', 'You'd better, or...', 'Stop that, or I'll...'

3. Moralising, preaching, imploring

   'What you really should do is...', 'You ought to...', 'It's your responsibility...'

4. Advising, giving suggestions or solutions

   'What I would do is...', 'Why don't you...?', 'Let me suggest...'

5. Persuading with logic, lecturing, arguing

   'Doesn't it make sense that if...', 'Here's where you're wrong...', 'The facts are...'

6. Judging, criticising, disagreeing, blaming

   'You aren't thinking clearly...', 'You have nobody to blame but yourself...', 'I couldn't disagree with you more...'

7. Praising, agreeing, evaluating positively, buttering up

   'I think you did exactly the right thing!', 'I couldn't agree more...', 'The same thing happened to me...'

8. Name-calling, ridiculing, shaming

   'You're worrying about nothing...', 'You always think...', 'Okay, know-it-all...'

9. Interpreting, analysing, diagnosing

   You're just trying to...', 'Your problem is...', 'You probably feel that way because...'

10. Reassuring, sympathising, consoling, supporting

    'Don't worry...', 'Look on the bright side...', 'Everyone goes through this...'

11. Probing, questioning, interrogating

    'Why did you do that?', 'And then what did you say?', 'Did you tell them...?'

12. Distracting, diverting, kidding

    'I'd rather not talk about it...', 'That's your problem...', 'You think you've got problems...'

A fifth, often misconceived, MI skill is *informing and advising*. Sometimes it is appropriate to provide information or offer advice, especially when helping people with HD/CD/ND to sort, organise and discard their belongings. Cognitive processing deficiencies, for example, may require us to help a client with decision-making or categorisation. However, in keeping with the spirit of MI, information or advice should be offered with permission and you should seek to fully understand the client's perspective and needs to help them reach their own decisions about whether your advice is relevant to them. Don't just offload your own views and opinions.

Developing discrepancy

As previously discussed, people with HD are often ambivalent or pre-contemplative about behaviour change, which can make it more difficult to engage in conversation, so this section focuses specifically on developing discrepancy which has always been a core element of MI.

Developing discrepancy highlights the gap between where we are now (status quo) and where we want to be (goal). It originates from Festinger's (1957) dissonance theory that cognitive dissonance exists when two or more conflicting beliefs or behaviours are held, for example wanting to be safe and secure at home but continuing to acquire and save items or making no attempt to sort and organise them and feeling despondent as a result.

Developing discrepancy seeks for us to, with respect and compassion but without judgement, 'hold a mirror', allowing the client to see the situation clearly and decide what, if anything, they want to do about it. Blaise Pascal (1623–1662) is quoted as saying, 'People are generally better persuaded by the reasons which they themselves have discovered than by those which have come into the mind of others'; that is to say, we usually prefer to believe our own reasons over the reasons of others.

Miller and Rollnick (2013) suggest three interconnected reasons for dissonance. In order to be motivating, a discrepancy should be *'lagom'* – a Swedish word for which there is no direct equivalent in English, meaning just so or not too much, not too little. The discrepancy should not be too small but should seem important enough to prompt action. Neither should it be too large nor feel too daunting. Discrepancy with a lack of self-efficacy will impact a person's motivation if they don't have confidence in their ability to affect change. If looking in the mirror evokes unpleasant experiences or memories, the person will want to avoid looking at those reflections, and if the discrepancy isn't *lagom* the situation is exacerbated.

To develop discrepancy, we must endeavour to create a safe environment for a client to feel able to 'look in the mirror'. A safe environment should have an atmosphere of acceptance and affirmation. It's only once the client accepts the situation that change becomes possible, but take heed – acceptance does not mean agreement! In the same way that whether we approve of the client's behaviour or not is irrelevant, we accept their inherent worth and see them as the unique individual they are. We affirm this by treating them with respect and compassion but without judgement.

Acceptance also requires us to honour the client's autonomy – their right to be and to choose. Personally, I have always adopted a 'live and let live' attitude to life and people. As long as a person doesn't cause harm to me or anyone else, they are free to live their life as they choose, because what right do I have to tell them otherwise? Also, saying 'You can't' to someone is probably going to evoke 'psychological reactance' (Brehm, 1966), meaning you are likely to receive negative reactions since they will feel as if their choices are being limited or taken away and they will want to reassert their free will.

Another aspect of acceptance is empathy. Showing empathy is to 'sense the client's inner world of private personal meanings as if it were your own, but without ever losing the "as if" quality' (Rogers 1959, p.210) or, put another way, stepping into their shoes (for a while). These are some ways to show empathy:

- Acknowledge the client's feelings: 'I'm sorry this is happening to you.'

- Express gratitude: 'Thank you for trusting me by telling me that; I'm grateful.'

- Be encouraging: 'You can do this. I believe in you.'

- Share your thoughts and feelings: 'I can't imagine what you must be going through.'

- Show interest: 'Am I right in thinking you feel frustrated by that?'

- Be supportive: 'How can I help?'

Affirming, conveying worth, respecting autonomy, and showing empathy will help to create an atmosphere of acceptance that is necessary to develop discrepancy in an authentically person-centred way.

Adopting an MI mindset and heart-set is essential throughout the process of instilling discrepancy, which is described by Miller and Rollnick as 'a process of sitting together and considering reasons why the person might contemplate change' (2013, p.248). In the spirit of MI, you would start by checking the client's knowledge and understanding of the situation. For example, you could ask, 'What do you know about the situation and why I'm here today?', but resist the temptation to respond with follow-up questions like 'So, why haven't you done anything about it?' because the client will likely become defensive and the conversation will go in the opposite direction to where you would like it to go. Instead, you could share with them what you know and understand about the circumstances. For example, you could ask, 'Do you mind if I check with you what I know?' or, 'Can I add a couple of points that you didn't mention to check that I understand correctly? Is that okay with you?' Then you could explore the client's reaction to what you just said by asking, 'What do you think?' or 'Does that make sense?'

In addition to OARS, there are some helpful strategies to evoke change talk. Change talk is 'any self-expressed language that is an argument for change' (Miller and Rollnick, 2013, pp.159–161). However, with ambivalence what we're also likely to hear, especially in early stages of the process, is sustain talk. In essence, this is both arguing for and against change and is a normal process that we all go through when trying to make a change.

Following collaborative work between Miller, Rollnick and the psycholinguist Amrhein (Amrhein *et al.*, 2003), two subtypes of change talk were identified: preparatory and mobilising – expressed using the mnemonics DARN CAT. Table 19.1: Talk for and against change shows examples of both subtypes using DARN CAT statements.

Table 19.1: Talk for and against change

	Change talk	Sustain talk
Preparatory		
Desire	I would like to get the boiler fixed.	I can cope without a boiler.
Ability	I could move some of the stuff from the hallway.	I can manage without a boiler.
Reason	It'll be winter soon and I don't want to be freezing cold.	I'll get one of those electric heaters.
Need	I need to speak to my landlord.	I don't need to get the landlord involved.
Mobilising		
Commitment	I could give the landlord a call.	I don't want to speak to the landlord.
Activation	I'll look out their phone number.	I don't think I've got the landlord's number anyway.
Taking steps	I'll find it before our next meeting and call them when you're here.	Even if I have the landlord's number, I'm not going to find it any time soon.

We can use OARS and DARN to ask evocative questions that explore change talk but be mindful of the need to hear a few preparatory statements before moving too quickly towards mobilising statements.

Desire for change

'How would you like things to change?

'What do you hope can be achieved by us working together?'

Ability to change

'If you did decide to create space in your bedroom, how could you do it?'

'What ideas do you have for how you could create space in your bedroom?'

Reason for change

'What could some of the advantages be of creating space in your bedroom?'

'What are the downsides of not being able to sleep in your bedroom?'

Need to change

'How serious or urgent does this feel to you?'

'What do you think has to change?'

Here are some other specific strategies.

Importance rulers

'On a scale from 0 to 10, how important is it to you to be able to sleep in your bed – where 0 is not at all important, and 10 is extremely important?

In following up ask:

'And why are you at...and not...[lower number than stated]?'

Asking why they're not at a higher number than stated will likely result in a sustain talk answer.

A similar approach could be to ask what answer a loved one might give to the same question, and then follow up with 'Why do you think their number is so high?'

Querying extremes

In the absence of desire for change you could explore the extremes of the situation and the consequences by asking:

'What are the worst things that might happen if you don't make this change?'

'What are the best things that might happen if you do make this change?'

Looking back

Ask about a time before the current situation arose:

'How were things better or different?

Looking forward

Ask what might happen if things continue as they are (status quo). You could ask the 'miracle' question:

'If you were 100 per cent successful in making the changes you want, what would be different? How would your life be this time next year, or in five years?'

Exploring goals and values

Ask about the client's own goals and values. What kind of life do they want to live? Using prompts like values cards could be useful for this exercise. If there is a 'problem' behaviour, for example excessive acquiring, difficulty discarding, or substance misuse, ask how that behaviour fits in with their stated goals or values.

Come alongside

Explicitly side with the negative (status quo) side of ambivalence.

'Perhaps...is so important to you that you won't give it up, no matter what the cost.'

Becoming proficient in motivational interviewing techniques requires a lot of practice. The skill is in knowing what to listen for as well as how to respond. Simultaneously use your OARS to direct the conversation and the DARN CAT to prepare and mobilise change talk.

CHAPTER 20

Harm-Reduction Approach

But what about those really challenging situations when there appears to be a lack of dissonance – when the client appears unconcerned about problematic hoarding and/or self-neglect behaviours? The very fact that you are having (or attempting to have) a conversation with them means there is a perceived need for some level of change, albeit instigated by a related professional, member of the community or a loved one. In all likelihood, you will have to consider a pragmatic harm-reduction approach to resolving risks and issues.

Harm reduction intervention services originated in The Netherlands in the 1970s (Busz *et al.*, 2024) and was then expanded on in the UK with the introduction of a comprehensive harm-reduction programme following the publication of the AIDS and Drug Misuse report from the Advisory Council on the Misuse of Drugs (ACMD, 1988). Psychologist and author Michael Tompkins adopted harm-reduction principles, values and assumptions which he applied to severe HD and used the term 'harm-reduction attitude' (2015a). As a quick aside, both *Digging Out* (Tompkins & Hartl 2009) and *Clinician's Guide to Severe Hoarding* (Tompkins 2015b) are also on my highly recommended reading list.

A harm-reduction attitude is a strategic approach rather than a specific individual treatment and requires us to:

- do no harm (carefully consider the risks and benefits of a clearout or relocation)

- not seek to eliminate the hoarding behaviour itself but to some degree decrease or mitigate associated risks and issues

- treat every individual client and their situation as unique

- include the client as an essential member of the harm-reduction team

- recognise that change is slow (and requires an MI mindset and heart-set)

- not see a single setback as a failure of the overall approach

- acknowledge that the client may have issues that seem more pressing to them and incorporate them into the harm-reduction plan.

A harm-reduction approach may be challenging for practitioners who like to conclude with an ending that allows them to 'tick a box' or say, 'job done' because this is a process that has a beginning (initial) and middle (ongoing), but no end in sight for as long as HD or self-neglect and related problems exist.

The initial phase of harm reduction is focused on assessing the level of risk and intervention, which is incorporated into the 'Explore circumstances and assessment' stage of the DESIRE method explored in Part Two. Therefore, I will mainly discuss the ongoing phase of harm reduction, but it would be remiss of me not to highlight that if during your initial conversations with the client as part of the engaging process, it becomes apparent to you that an intervention will be necessary and imminent (i.e. if the client's home is severely cluttered and there are signs of self-neglect, public or environmental health risks, little or no insight into the problem and refusal to receive help and support from housing, health and social care or third-sector service providers), you discuss the severity of the situation and allude to a strategic harm-reduction approach.

> When a person with HD lacks insight or motivation and ignores or avoids dealing with associated risks and issues, adopting a 'harm reduction attitude' is the most helpful approach. Poor insight often results in a lack of awareness about the implications of their accumulated possessions and rejecting offers of help. Emotional attachment to their belongings may be difficult to overcome, and fear of stigma and societal judgment lead to further social isolation and avoidance of the issue. (Bratiotis, Muroff, & Lin, 2021, p.400)

These can be very difficult conversations to have and may be overwhelming for both the client and practitioner. You are likely to need your whole panoply of skills so, with your MI mindset and heart-set, use your OARS, bring the DARN CAT and deploy anything else that works for you that will help to minimise any 'future shock'.

The ongoing phase involves initiation, engagement, assessment of harm, building the harm-reduction team, planning and ongoing management. Let's consider each of these in turn and I will outline how we (Life-Pod) would approach this phase.

Initiation

Where the client referral comes from will impact how and when you respond but regardless of source, I and my team would never visit a client's home without their prior knowledge and permission. Instead, I would ask the referrer to let the client know about Life-Pod – perhaps provide them with information about our organisation or seek their permission for us to get in touch with them. I always stress the importance of them advising a client that we do not endorse enforced clearouts so we're not going to remove any of their belongings from their home without their permission and that even if they allow us to visit or speak with them, they are under no obligation to work with us – it is entirely their choice. All we would want a client to know at this stage is that we understand the complexities of clutter-related conditions and our key aim is to help them to avoid eviction, return home from hospital, resolve any public or environmental health issues, and generally make them safer and relatively more comfortable at home. Sadly, in cases of Diogenes syndrome (self-neglect or domestic squalor), clients are often told at this stage that working with an organisation like Life-Pod is their only option, but we see this as an opportunity to make our coerced help as unproblematic and undemanding an experience as possible for the client.

Engagement

At a first meeting with a client our objective is purely to introduce ourselves and reinforce the messages we asked the referrer to relay previously. We wish to spend time with the client and get a feel for the situation, listen to their views and concerns, and reassure them of our intentions and approach. At this point in the process, we're not necessarily concerned with writing notes, filling in forms or doing any formal assessment; all we need to do is establish whether the situation raises any potential safeguarding issues and to listen. Adam Kahane discerned that 'the way to listen is to stop talking' (Kahane, 2007, p.113). We must avoid guessing how the client feels and instead aim to actually find out by asking the right type of questions and actively listening to their answers. Our hope is that before we leave, we get the client's agreement to come back for a follow-up assessment meeting in the very near future. In more than a decade, I am pleased that I need only one hand to count the number of people who after a first engagement meeting have not gone on to work with me and latterly my team.

Assessment of harm

Diogenes syndrome is often considered to be a safeguarding issue. Again, there will be specific legislation to cover this from your local government but in Scotland it is managed in accordance with the Adult Support and Protection (Scotland) Act 2007 (Scottish Government, 2022). The Act is the primary health and social care legislative framework designed to protect those adults (a person aged 16 years or over) who are unable to safeguard their own interests and are at risk of harm because they are affected by disability, mental disorder, illness or physical or mental infirmity. Harm means all harm, including self-harm and neglect.

The Act defines an 'adult at risk' as someone who meets all of the following three-point criteria:

- They are unable to safeguard their own wellbeing, property, rights, or other interests.

- They are at risk of harm.

- Because they are affected by disability, mental disorder, illness or physical or mental infirmity they are more vulnerable to being harmed than adults who are not so affected.

A word I hear often from related professionals, especially those in health and social care, when discussing hoarding and self-neglect is 'capacity', so it's also worth highlighting how the Act deals with capacity:

It should be noted and strongly emphasized that the three-point criteria above make no reference to capacity. For the purposes of the Act, capacity should be considered on a contextual basis around a specific decision, and not restricted to an overall clinical judgement. It is recognized that, due to many factors in an individual's life, capacity to make an authentic decision is a fluctuating concept. Thus, even if deemed to possess general capacity, attention must be paid to whether a person has clear decisional and executional ability (i.e., to both make and action decisions) to safeguard themselves in the specific context arising. (Scottish Government, 2022, p.15)

As well as capacity, there is also the matter of a person's ability and willingness to protect themselves, their home, their rights, and other interests. The Act covers this too:

Most people will be able to safeguard themselves through the ability to take clear and well thought through decisions about matters to do with their health and safety, and as such could not be regarded as adults at risk of harm within the terms of the Act.

However, this will not be the case for all people, and when a person is deemed unable to safeguard themselves, they will meet the first point of the three-point criteria [...]. 'Unable' is not further defined in the Act but is defined in the Collins English Dictionary as 'lacking the necessary power, ability, or authority (to do something); not able'.

'Unwilling' is defined in the Collins English Dictionary as 'unfavourably inclined; reluctant' and may thus describe someone who is aware of the potential consequences but still makes a deliberate choice.

A distinction may therefore be drawn between an adult who lacks these skills and is therefore unable to safeguard themselves, and one who is deemed to have the power, ability, or authority to safeguard themselves, but who is apparently unwilling to do so. (Scottish Government, 2022, p.15)

As ever, the devil is in the detail, and I think it's this additional 'Note' below that is often the point of contention when it comes to decisions made in relation to hoarding and self-neglect. I believe that the development and implementation of national guidelines for hoarding and self-neglect would alleviate contentious issues and influence safeguarding outcomes.

Note: An adult who is considered unwilling to safeguard themselves, rather than unable to safeguard themselves, may not be considered an adult at risk.

This distinction requires careful consideration. All adults who have capacity have the right to make their own choices about their lives and these choices should be respected if they are made freely. However, for many people the effects of trauma and/or adverse childhood experiences may impact upon both their ability to make and action decisions, and the type of choices they appear to make. In this context it is reasonable to envisage situations in which these experiences, and the cumulative impact of them through life, may very well have rendered some people effectively unable, through reliable decision making or action, to safeguard themselves. (Scottish Government, 2022, p.15)

Harm-reduction team

This is often a challenging juncture when trying to resolve severe hoarding-related problems. Not least because this is when resources will be discussed, and some people will want to seek a quick resolution with minimal expenditure. Also, there is always the risk with so many stakeholders involved that the client's voice goes unheard or is disregarded. In Scotland, Adult Support and Protection practice procedures (Scottish Government, 2022) state that committees should be 'multi-agency and multi-disciplinary'; each of whom will bring their own agenda and priorities to the table. Harm-reduction teams will most likely involve professionals from fire and safety, police, public and environmental health, housing, health and social care. They should also involve the client and ideally another person to represent them, for example a friend or family member, advocacy or support worker.

Once the team members have been identified, the next step is to clarify the problem and agree an intervention plan. Each discipline is likely to have their own way of capturing information, and as a former project manager I use familiar tools known by the acronyms SPIN and BOSCARD – neither of which are typically used in this field, but I believe are useful for capturing relevant information for all stakeholders irrespective of discipline.

SPIN is useful as a one-pager to capture high-level information:

- **Situation** – gather relevant information from all team members.

- **Problem** – highlight all the risks and issues that have been raised.

- **Implication** – state why these risks and issues must be resolved.

- **Need** – agree what needs to happen, when it needs to happen and who is responsible for resolving each individual risk or issue.

BOSCARD is a more detailed process of capturing all the information required before implementing an intervention plan.

- **Background** – outline problems that necessitate a harm-reduction approach.

- **Objective** – define overall objective and specific goals for achieving it.

- **Scope** – describe the overall result to be achieved from the intervention.

- **Constraints** – identify specific limitations or conditions placed on the intervention.

- **Assumptions** – specify all known factors that should be considered.

- **Risks** – outline any risks identified and ways to mitigate them.

- **Deliverables** – define the outcomes to be achieved, by whom and when.

Coming back to resources, in their report, *Beyond Overwhelmed*, the San Francisco Task Force on Compulsive Hoarding (2009, p.2) 'conservatively estimate that costs to service providers and landlords from compulsive hoarding are $6.43 million a year. The incalculable human cost in the lives of individuals and families adds significantly to these financial impacts.' Other studies state that without ongoing assistance, most people who accept that clearouts will happen soon begin to hoard again, and even with ongoing assistance, the problem over time tends to reappear, and sometimes worsens (Frost, Steketee & Williams, 2000; Kim, Steketee & Frost, 2001). But we mustn't overlook the moral costs associated with HD. Michael Tompkins, psychologist and member of the San Francisco Task Force on Compulsive Hoarding, highlighted in his book, *Clinician's Guide to Severe Hoarding – A Harm Reduction Approach*:

> Landlords across San Francisco evict between 400 and 800 people with HD from their homes and threaten to evict another 1200–2400 each year. Many of those forced from their [homes] are older adults who have suffered with the problem for decades. Now, frail and in failing health, they are removed from their [home] at a time when physically and psychologically they are the most vulnerable. Removing frail older adults from a [home] in which they may have lived 30 or more years and relocating them to another setting devoid of their possessions is a devastating outcome. (Tompkins, 2015b, p.9)

Regardless of how you plan an intervention the subject of resources will drive many decisions and we know that severe hoarding and self-neglect are resource-intensive problems. We also know that enforced clearouts are not efficient or effective and can have catastrophic results. But sometimes there is no other option than to clear a property where there are significant public health, environmental or structural risks and issues that must be addressed, which can often be the case, especially where self-neglect is present. However, if at all possible, we should consider what Tompkins terms a 'modified' cleanout and remove only what is necessary from the home, salvaging as many of the client's possessions as is feasible. Reassuring the client that this is the plan and allowing them the opportunity to identify specific items they are especially keen to keep is more likely to gain their acceptance of and compliance with the situation.

Planning and prioritising

Assessment of the situation will undoubtedly lead to a long list of actions and each agency will have a different set of priorities specific to their own profession. A modified harm-reduction plan should agree specific actions to be taken and improvements made to decrease the harm potential of the client and any other occupants within the home or neighbouring properties.

Another planning technique I often use for prioritisation is one I have adapted from the MoSCoW method, developed in 1994 by software developer Dai Clegg. The acronym stands for Must, Should, Could and Would; the Os don't stand for anything and are usually in lowercase with the sole purpose of creating a pronounceable word. This is a useful method to reach consensus on the most pressing needs and to gain an understanding of the wider implications.

In practice, the multi-agency harm-reduction team together would brainstorm problems, risks and issues to be resolved, and then work through the list to reach a consensus on the priorities. Each item listed is considered based on agreed criteria. Below are some examples only, since each situation is unique and should be assessed and prioritised as such:

- **Must do** – critical and requires urgent intervention (e.g. specific risk to public health; means of ingress and egress).

- **Should do** – important but not posing an immediate risk (e.g. utility repairs; fire and safety risks).

117

- **Could do** – necessary to minimise potential risk (e.g. create safe spaces to cook, eat and wash).

- **Would do** – improve daily living activities (e.g. reorganise/dismantle stacks of heavy boxes).

Applying the MoSCoW method to the example actions above might look like this:

Would

- Transfer items from plastic bags and flimsy cardboard boxes into more sturdy storage boxes.

- Ensure items are stored safely and stacked in such a way to avoid easily toppling over.

Must

- Arrange for pest control services to implement rodent control to treat and eliminate the pest population from the home.

- Move existing clutter away from the ingress and egress doorways so that they can open fully, and ensure that they remain a clutter-free area.

Should

- Empty food waste into a bin and empty it into the outside collection bins at least once a week.

- Resolve electrical risks caused by multiple overloaded sockets and extension cables.

Could

- Clear clutter off the bed, or from an identified space on the floor so the client can fully lie down horizontally to promote better sleep.

- Replace bed linen with flame-retardant bedding and avoid smoking in bed to reduce fire risk.

Of course, available resources will significantly impact the decisions made and a multi-agency approach could pool resources and make best use of the required skills, knowledge and expertise.

CASE STUDY: CHRISTMAS SPIRIT

70-year-old, homeowner-occupier

C lived alone in a detached four-bedroom cottage with separate garage and front and rear garden. C had lived experience of HD, which intensified following the death of both of her parents. In her late 60s, C's hoarding behaviours got significantly worse and developed to include self-neglect.

C had started sleeping in her car because her home was no longer easily accessible or habitable and one evening, between Christmas and New Year, C was found by a police officer in her car and, because the engine was running (to provide heat) and C was drinking alcohol, she was subsequently charged with a criminal offence. In the days that followed, C was hospitalised following a significant breakdown in her physical and mental health.

Although C's home had become uninhabitable and there were environmental health issues, including human waste, pest infestations and bio-hazard materials inside the home, no 'public health' concerns had been raised and, although malodourous on approach, outwardly the home was no different from any of the others in the street.

I was contacted by a health and social care professional who asked if I would be willing to help C by making her home safe to return to and once she was discharged from hospital, provide ongoing assistance to manage her clutter and belongings. At that time, we had not envisaged C would remain in a hospital facility for 12 months before returning home.

The first thing I did was arrange to meet with C in the hospital. I was aware she had previously experienced a clearout and because it had been a distressing experience, she was reluctant to agree to it happening again. I reassured her that I would salvage as many of her belongings as possible without putting anyone at risk. We discussed that due to bio-hazard materials, I would have to involve specialist cleaners to remove some items. C was quite poorly, and her symptoms included both bowel and urinary incontinence that resulted in her bedroom and bathroom being filled with soiled items. There was also a plumbing issue that caused the bath to fill and overflow with dirty water that spread into the hallway and soaked clothes, books and food that had been stored there.

With an over-arching plan to make C's home safe to return to and then for us to work together on sorting, organising and decluttering her belongings once she was home, C gave me permission to carry out the work in her home on the agreement that I would also oversee the work being carried out by specialist extreme cleaners and a plumber. I also agreed that I would do my utmost to find and salvage several items that C had listed – for example, a box containing her late mother's jewellery that she believed to be in the bathroom. Due to the volume and nature of items, I sought permission from C to hire a skip to be placed alongside her home; we hired a total of three skips to completion. I estimated it would take between seven and ten days to sort, clear and deep-clean C's home and have the plumbing repairs carried out. I told C I would call her at the end of each day to provide a progress report and we could discuss any queries or issues that arose.

On the first day working in C's home, I was surprised to discover that upstairs housed two double bedrooms with an adjoining 'Jack and Jill' ensuite cloakroom, all of which were largely uncluttered. My initial thought was to wonder why C had taken to sleeping in her car instead of upstairs, but I quickly remembered I'd had to clear the area around the bottom of the stairs to gain access, which C had been unable to do. Finding the space upstairs allowed me to box up items that could be kept and move them up into those rooms, thus creating space downstairs to enable the specialist extreme cleaners to clear all bio-hazard and contaminated items.

When clearing the bedroom, it became obvious that C's bed was unsalvageable so, as this was an item on her list of things she wanted to keep, when I called at the end of the day we discussed it and C agreed to let it go and we sourced a new bed for her. There was also a very large and heavy old TV in the sitting room as well as a new one still in its box. Rather than assume it was a replacement and put the old one in the skip, I asked C what she wanted us to do, which helped to build trust and reinforce the fact that she was in control of any decisions being made.

C was very fond of Christmas as it evoked special memories of times spent with her parents and she had one window in her home that was decorated year-round with a long garland with berries. While I was working in and around the home, a neighbour stopped and asked, 'When are you going to remove that crap from the window?', to which I replied, 'Never' since again, it was on the list of things C wanted to keep and remain untouched, along with contents inside cupboards and drawers.

To complete the project, it took two extreme cleaners three days, one plumber half a day, and me six days, at a cost of approximately £6,500. I had achieved what I wanted to do, which was to make the house safe for

C to return to and it still resembling her home. The hospital had arranged for C to visit her home while I was there so she could see the progress made. She was overjoyed and a little emotional.

While in hospital as part of her treatment plan, C started to participate in bereavement therapy but didn't continue with it as she felt it to be too painful. While attending a 'case conference' meeting with the health and social care team involved in C's care as part of her discharge plan, I raised a cautionary flag that unresolved grief may result in the continuance of hoarding behaviours. C had been on some 'shopping trips' with friends who had visited her at the hospital facility (mental health rehabilitation accommodation) and had acquired new items that she brought back to the accommodation, indicating that acquiring and saving was quite likely to continue once she was home. However, it was agreed that once home, since I would meet with C fortnightly (as per the previously agreed plan) to help declutter her belongings, this would provide the opportunity to monitor and assess ongoing acquiring and saving habits.

Once home, C and I had several sessions working through her belongings and while she did continue to acquire new things, it was on a much smaller scale and slower pace.

About two years after I stopped visiting C she became ill again and had taken to spending most of her days in bed, with her incontinence once again an issue. However, C called me before her situation got too bad and I helped her once again. I also encouraged her to seek help from her doctor, which she did, and eventually she discovered that the combined medication she was taking was causing bowel and bladder issues. Once that was resolved, C returned home and was able to better manage her hoarding behaviours.

CHAPTER 21

Transdisciplinary Case Management Approach

Some organisations, especially housing and community-based service providers, may find a case management approach helpful in supporting their clients with problematic clutter-related issues. A study by Bratiotis, Woody and Lauster (2019) stated that 'case management consists of a set of well-established strategies commonly used in community service settings to address serious mental illness and similar complex problems' (p.93) and reviewed how four organisations used case management as a hoarding intervention approach. These activities involved:

- **supportive relationship** – essential to establish and maintain working relationship

- **assessment** – identify severity, risks, and issues; agree priority actions

- **goal-setting** – use strategies to set SMART goals

- **brokering and linking** – with multi-agency, multi-disciplinary, community-based organisations

- **teaching and modelling** – develop skills and abilities to maintain secure tenancy

- **monitoring** – sometimes maintain an ongoing relationship (and always be ready to re-engage if necessary).

A report (Richardson *et al.*, 2014) based on research jointly commissioned by the Chartered Institute of Housing (CIH) and Wheatley Group[1] stated:

---

1   Wheatley Group is the UK's largest builder of social rented homes and one of Scotland's leading care providers (www.wheatley-group.com).

'the housing frontline is changing' and outlined some 'core characteristics' and 'qualities that people in these roles need to possess', namely:

- **differentiated** – using data intelligence to guide how officer time is used, rather than providing a blanket service for all residents

- **relational** – doing things with residents, rather than doing things to or for them

- **interactive** – working alongside professionals from other disciplines to achieve a broader range of outcomes for residents

- **varied and creative** – finding solutions, even if they lie outside of 'normal activity'

- **engaged and impactful** – doing things with the intention of having a positive impact on people's lives and the organisation's bottom line

- **novel and anticipatory** – doing something now to avoid negative consequences later on. (p.2)

Placed alongside each other and with the synergies between them (as illustrated in Table 21.1), it's easy to see how a case management approach to managing excessive clutter-related risks and issues could be integrated with the 'new era' of frontline roles in housing management, and how the DESIRE method supports them both.

Table 21.1: Case management, new era housing management and DESIRE

Case management	Frontline futures	DESIRE
Supportive relationship	Relational	Determine cause and effect
Assessment	Differentiated	Establish circumstances and assessment
Goal-setting	Varied and creative	Seek therapeutic intervention
Brokering and linking	Interactive	Implement the plan
Teaching and modelling	Engaged and impactful	
Monitoring	Novel and anticipatory	Review and evaluate

I believe that an opportunity exists for housing professionals to take a lead role in transdisciplinary working as a way to manage risks and issues related to extreme clutter and hoarding disorder. Certainly, when delivering training courses, frontline housing professionals have shown a great deal of skill and empathy as well as a desire to help their clients avoid risk of eviction, and show a genuine concern for their overall health and wellbeing.

Transdisciplinary working involves members of the multi-agencies working collaboratively, sharing objectives, responsibilities and delivery of outcomes. A published paper (Salama & Alshuwaikhat, 2006) on the subject of using a transdisciplinary approach in relation to sustainable affordable housing stated:

> Trans-disciplinarity is a new form of learning and problem-solving involving cooperation among different parts of society and academia in order to meet complex challenges of society. Trans-disciplinary research starts from tangible, real-world problems. Solutions are devised in collaboration with multiple stakeholders. Thus, trans-disciplinarity is about transgressing boundaries of disciplines.

> As a practice-oriented approach, trans-disciplinarity is not confined to a closed circle of scientific experts, professional journals, and academic departments where knowledge is produced. Through mutual learning, the knowledge of all participants is enhanced. The sum of this knowledge will be greater than the knowledge of any single partner. In the process, the bias of each perspective will also be minimized (Klein, 1998; Klein *et al.*, 2001). (p.41)

It has indeed been my experience that when delivering training courses attended by multi-agency professionals, they seem to learn as much from each other as they do from me in terms of managing extreme clutter-hoarding.

A different study (Gibb *et al.*, 2009) relating to transdisciplinary working in the development of health and social care provision in mental health, reported 'evident benefits for team members, management and service users' (p.339) and feedback from study participants, who formed a collaborative working group, identified the following positive outcomes of working together (p.347):

- A sense of common purpose.

- More efficient inter-agency communication pathways.

- A more efficient and flexible service, increasing the responsiveness of the service to clients, allowing team members to manage 'red tape' more effectively.

- An increase in staff morale resulting from a decrease in isolation.

- A good level of team support through the availability and willingness of team members to share with and listen to each other.

- Joint training opportunities.

A case management approach is not dissimilar to the proposed concept of establishing a team approach and cooperation between agencies when meeting individual need through a care management model for the implementation of the UK National Health Service and Community Care Act (Department of Health & Social Security, 1990; Couchman, 1995).

In the current climate, all related professions are under immense pressure due to diminishing resources, increasing numbers in the older generation and a lack of social housing stock. There are additional pressures on housing, health and social care services, the attention given to the client-centredness and the need for a greater focus on prevention and early intervention.

It seems logical to me that housing providers, who already have an existing and ongoing relationship with clients and who are changing their role in 'new era housing management', will have, or should be developing, the necessary skills, qualities and capabilities to lead the way in adopting a new transdisciplinary case management approach to helping people with lived experience of hoarding and chronic disorganisation.

Still, whichever profession a helper is affiliated to they will, I hope, find the resources in Part Four useful when it comes to helping clients to implement their agreed change plans.

Part Four

IMPLEMENT THE PLANNED INTERVENTION

LEARNING OBJECTIVE

Having considered key elements of professional practice in addition to best practice tools and techniques, it is expected the reader will be able to support the development and implementation of an outcomes-focused plan.

CHAPTER 22

Ethical Practice

Intervention is sometimes influenced by social norms that can foster preconceived ideas about socially acceptable ways of living, including our belongings. I think norms and standards relating to the quantity and presentation of belongings in our homes across different cultures is an interesting topic but research to date is very limited. A project for another day perhaps! For now, referring back to my opening comments, we are not necessarily trying to 'conquer' clutter – we're working to resolve risks and issues while focusing on the client's health, safety and wellbeing. However, before we look at the ways in which we can help, there are some areas for consideration that affect how, why and what you say or do.

Practitioners 'provide invaluable services by enhancing motivation, providing support, and providing manual labour; however, they introduce [an] area for ethical dilemmas to occur' (Gibson *et al.*, 2010, p.427). Ethical practice is an area I feel strongly about and is the driving force behind Life-Pod and my ambition to advance the Hoarding Academy to an institute. Hoarding is complex and specialist practitioners should have the necessary skills and knowledge required to help those affected by the disorder; they will inevitably encounter situations that require them to respond but they should maintain professional ethical and moral values. At Life-Pod, we refer to an ethical practice framework for guidance in response to ethical issues or dilemmas. The framework upholds our professional standards, shapes our client relationships and informs our practice. Our ethics underpin our purpose and actions, which are based on our values:

- **Pragmatism** – we provide resourceful solutions that can be implemented in a practical and insightful way.

- **Compassion** – we listen to understand the needs and wants of our clients and always adopt a harm-reduction attitude.

129

- **Collaboration** – we partner with clients and related professionals to achieve shared goal-oriented outcomes.

- **Pioneering** – we explore new and innovative ways of doing things in order to create 'fit for purpose' and accessible solutions.

Our values include a commitment to:

- respecting human rights and dignity

- enhancing people's safety and wellbeing capabilities

- improving the quality of relationships between people and their community

- increasing personal resilience and effectiveness

- recognising and appreciating cultural and human diversity

- ensuring the integrity of practitioner–client relationships

- enhancing the quality of professional knowledge and its application

- striving for the fair and adequate provision of services.

I wholeheartedly believe that no one should face judgement because of the way they were born, where they come from, what they believe or whether they have a disability. The UK Government's Equality Act 2010 (Gov.uk, 2013) defines a disability as a physical or mental condition that has a long-term, adverse effect on your day-to-day life and states that service providers must not discriminate by treating disabled people less favourably than non-disabled people, and must make reasonable adjustments to their services. So, in addition to ethical and moral practice, we must also adhere to legislative obligations when helping people whose chronic and severe clutter-related problems negatively impact their daily living activities.

An equally important part of our role is to ensure that clients know what help and support is available to them and to advocate on their behalf and communicate with related professionals and other members of their community, including their loved ones and support providers who may also need to be aware of and informed about HD, CD or ND and symptomatic clutter.

CASE EXAMPLES: ADVOCACY

Over the years, there have been many times when I have advocated on behalf of clients in a variety of circumstances. Here are some examples:

- A client who, following her mother's death, was bequeathed her family home where she had lived her entire life with both of her parents, received an inheritance tax bill from the UK HM Revenues and Customs (HMRC). Aged around 70, the client had no savings and no regular income and therefore was unable to pay the bill, so HMRC wanted her to 'liquidise the asset' in order to generate funds to pay the debt. The client sought legal advice and later, once the lawyer had been to the home and discovered the volume of belongings and size of the challenge to make it 'market ready', they contacted me seeking help for the situation. It seemed cruel to me and unnecessary to force an older person to sell their home – the only one they had ever lived in – and she had no other living relatives she could in turn leave the home to. The lawyer agreed and, in an effort to urge HMRC to consider alternative options, I spoke with the client's doctor and, on making them aware of HD, asked if they would be willing to provide a formal diagnosis (post *DSM-5* publication but pre-*ICD-11* implementation) for the client, which they were not. In absence of a formal diagnosis, I wrote a 'supporting statement' for the client which her lawyer submitted to HMRC along with a request to allow the client to remain in her home until her death, at which point the property would be sold and the HMRC bill would be paid in full. Thankfully, they agreed.

- Another client, aged around 40, had her child removed from the home by Children & Families Services due to concerns about the child's welfare, including health and safety issues resulting from the mother's (client) lived experience of HD, symptoms of self-neglect and drug misuse. While working with the client and since we were making good progress, she asked if I would be willing to attend the next meeting of the Children's Hearing Panel to tell them about the work we were doing together to make the home a safer place to live. She wished me to advise them that she had been able to let go of some belongings thus making the child's bedroom, living room and hallway clutter-free and clean. I was happy to do so, and in fact attended two Children's Hearing Panel meetings with her over a six-month period but unfortunately, due to the decision by panel members not to allow the child to return home as yet, the client became angry and frustrated, leading to further drug misuse and disengagement from our work. This was sad but outside my control and area of expertise to be able to help the client further.

- I had been contacted by a client who was the third generation of her family to be living in her home under a secured tenancy. The local authority wanted to upgrade the kitchen in the property and during a visit to the home the housing officer stated there was 'too much stuff and it would have to be removed'. The client asked if I would visit her home at the same time as the next scheduled visit from the housing officer. When I arrived, the client, who is elderly and has mobility problems, was in tears while listening to the housing officer admonishing her and saying, 'You are lucky we [housing provider] let you stay in this house.' At which point I asked, 'Is there any need for that...can you not see you're upsetting [the client]?' I gave the client a tissue and a hug and reassured her it would be okay and then suggested to the housing officer we start again and have a chat about the situation and what we needed to do to enable the work to go ahead as planned.

CHAPTER 23

Language and Communication

The language we use – both spoken and non-spoken – is important. Language has a strong influence on thought, and 'habitual uses of language can influence our habit of thought and action' (Lumen, 2024). Therefore, how we talk about hoarding or neurodivergence is inextricably linked to how we think about it and our actions as a result. 'In the context of mental illness, mental health, and wellbeing, negative words can be experienced as condescending, isolating, and stigmatising, whereas positive words can convey dignity, empathy, and hope' (Richards, 2018). In 2017, the Royal College of Psychiatrists published a report that articulated their eight core values: communication, dignity, empathy, fairness, honesty, humility, respect and trust (Richards & Lloyd, 2017). They wanted to reinforce the principle that these values shape the language and terminology used by their profession to provide person-centred mental healthcare.

As a veteran communications professional, I would summarise good communication as being unambiguous and respectful; using effective listening and evocative questioning skills to set the tone and flow of a positive conversation, irrespective of the medium. With the odd exception, most TV and media depictions of people with lived experience HD are derogatory and distasteful. Japanese media refer to hoarding behaviour as *gomi-yashiki*, meaning rubbish (*gomi*) house (*yashiki*). Holmes *et al.* (2015) recommended that 'the national media should seek advice from experts…about the portrayal of people with hoarding problems and desist from using mental health problems to entertain and shock the public'. As a professional who chooses to work in this field, I believe I have a responsibility not only to raise awareness of HD and ND but also to de-stigmatise disorders in the hope we can encourage more people with lived experience to ask for and receive appropriate help. Some of the ways we can do this are by being mindful of the language we use and by challenging others' misconceptions, including journalists, presenters and related professionals. I never have and never will use the term 'hoarder' – even if a client I am working with describes themselves that way, I don't accept that as permission for me to do so.

In the book titled *Understanding Hoarding* (Cooke, 2017), the author included a 'note: for people who hoard, their families and friends' that starts by saying: 'It's important to be sensitive in our use of language when talking about hoarding, and we need to use terminology that respects individuals' dignity and avoids labelling them' and ends with: 'However, when referring to someone who hoards, for the sake of brevity and clarity I have also respectfully used "hoarder", a term which is in common usage and person-centred' (Cooke, 2017, p.x). I believe this is an oxymoron: you can't show sensitivity and avoid labelling someone if you consciously choose to call them a 'hoarder' because it's easier, simpler or more concise. Neither does it provide clarity since the label encourages us to focus on a person's behaviour rather than their mental illness. Historically, terms like 'retard', 'loony' and 'cripple' were commonly used but we now acknowledge they are derogatory and disrespectful. And with the best will in the world, using labels to describe people affected by a complex mental disorder can never be deemed person-centred. Psychiatric research shows that 'the internalized stigma of mental illness impedes recovery and is associated with increased depression, reduced self-esteem, reduced recovery orientation, reduced empowerment, and increased perceived devaluation and discrimination' (Boyd, Otilingam & DeForge, 2014, p.17).

As well as how we talk about people, we should also be aware of how we talk about their belongings. Avoid using pejoratives like 'junk', 'hoard', 'rubbish' and aim to mirror the client's language by listening for what terms they use and inject them in your conversations. And equally important, always ask permission before touching or moving a client's possessions. It's unlikely that you will have to do this continuously but especially at the start of your working relationship it's a good way to build trust and show respect.

CHAPTER 24

Strengths-Based Approach

The origin of Life-Pod's name relates to 'Life' (ways of living, capacity for growth and transformation), and 'Pod', which is an acronym for **P**lan (to think about and decide what you are going to do, or how you are going to do something), **O**rganise (to do or arrange things, plans, ideas, etc., according to a particular system so that they can be used or understood easily) and **D**evelop (to grow or cause to grow and change into a more motivated, skilled and able individual).

Our *wholistic* client-centred practice means we use a variety of tools, techniques and approaches in the course of our work, selecting the most appropriate based on need and circumstance. Whereas previously during the engagement process, we were largely looking back, the planning stage allows us to look forward and explore the client's hopes and aspirations for how they want to live their life. First, spend time getting to know the client and aim to understand what concerns they may have or what challenges they are facing. Recognise that they themselves are likely to have within them what is required. Bring your professional curiosity to the fore and with kindness and compassion ask about the client's aspirations, values and strengths.

We adopt a strengths-based approach that, although originated in social care, can be applied across multi-disciplines that have a role that involves provision of help and support for a client.

When using a strengths-based approach, risk is looked at as an enabler, not as a barrier. Risks should be explored with the individual and from their point of view. The role of the professional is not solely to 'reduce risks' but to support the individual in managing risks. This can be done by:

- identifying all the potential benefits and potential risks of a particular activity or decision for the individual and others

- exploring and fully understanding the consequences of both the potential benefits and the potential risks for them and others

- collaboratively, identifying the best way to manage the identified risks, maximising the benefits and if appropriate reducing the potential negative consequences. (Baron & Stanley, 2019, p.25)

We can use MI strategies to identify and explore risks, issues and behaviours, and adopt a harm-reduction attitude to help manage the risks and minimise negative consequences when implementing a strengths-based approach. Below are some examples of strength-based questions:

Get to know the client:

- What are you most proud of in your life?

- What inspires you and gives you energy?

- What support have you received previously that you found helpful?

- What does a good day look like for you? What makes it a good day?

Find out about the client's strengths:

- What would people who know you say you're good at doing?

- How did you become good at doing that?

- What are you most proud of about yourself?

- What would the people closest to you describe as your superpower?

Find out about the client's hopes:

- What would you like to get out of our work together?

- What would be happening if things were better for you right now?

- What are the things in your life that you really value?

- What are your hopes, dreams and aspirations?

Using 'values cards' is also a good way to help identify what is important to a client and to explore their beliefs and aspirations. Our personal value systems, which are formed from factors such as culture, childhood, education and experiences, underpin our attitudes and behaviours, which can be 'partly or wholly unconscious' (Vyskocilova *et al.*, 2015, p.41), so clarifying personal values can be useful for both client and practitioner. Examples of values are:

- **acceptance** – to be open to and accepting of myself, others, life, and so on

- **courage** – to be courageous or brave in the face of fear, threat or difficulty

- **ccology** to live in harmony with the environment

- **fitness** – to maintain or improve my fitness; to look after my physical and mental health and wellbeing

- **flexibility** – to adjust and adapt readily to changing circumstances

- **gratitude** – to be grateful for and appreciative of the positive aspects of life

- **honesty** – to be honest, truthful and sincere with myself and others

- **independence** – to be self-supportive and choose my own way of doing things

- **knowledge** – to learn and contribute valuable skills and knowledge

- **order** – to be orderly and organised

- **self-control** – to act in accordance with my own ideals

- **spirituality** – to connect with things bigger than myself

- **tolerance** – to accept and respect those who differ from me.

CHAPTER 25

Setting Goals and Outcomes

When we set goals for ourselves that align with our values, we're more intrinsically motivated to work hard to reach them, so getting to know more about what's important to our clients is necessary when helping them to set aspiring and achievable goals. There are different types of goals, but I believe the most helpful for clients with HD/CD/ND are those based on behaviour and outcomes. Behaviour-based goals aim to change how you think and act as a result of certain circumstances; results-based goals focus on achieving actions within specified parameters. The skill is in the integration of the two: using OARS to focus on the client's strengths is key to being outcomes-focused, and using strengths-based questions will help to facilitate the flow of conversation.

There are two widely used strategies for setting outcomes or goals, known by the acronyms WOOP and SMART. WOOP stands for Wish, Outcome, Obstacle and Plan, and may be useful for people who prefer to work with thoughts and imagery. SMART stands for Specific, Measurable, Achievable, Relevant and Time-bound and is perhaps more suitable for people who prefer to use rational or effortful thinking strategies.

WOOP

Answers to the following questions can help to define WOOP outcomes:

Wish – What is your wish? Does it feel challenging but achievable?

Outcome – What would be the outcome of that wish coming true? How would fulfilling your wish make you feel? [Visualisation exercise: Keep your thoughts at the front of your mind and give them free rein to vividly imagine the outcome.]

Obstacle – What obstacle(s) (internal or external) may stand in the way of you achieving your wish? What emotion or behaviour of yours could prevent you from fulfilling your wish? [Visualisation exercise: Keep your thoughts and feelings at the front of your mind as you imagine the obstacle that is in your way.]

Plan – What can you do to overcome the obstacle(s)? Identify the action you can take or the thought you can react to as a way to overcome your obstacle.

An example WOOP goal might be:

(*Wish*) I want to sleep in my bed. (*Outcome*) I will be less tired, have more energy and be able to achieve more. (*Obstacle*) I have so many other important things I need to do. (*Plan*) I will schedule 15 minutes each day to work on clearing stuff from my bed. I will deal with one item at a time to avoid churning and wasting time.

And an add-on that may help to prevent or overcome obstacles:

If [obstacle] then I will [action/thought to prevent/overcome your obstacle].

If I start churning, I will take a break and think about how better I will feel once I am able to sleep in my bed.

SMART

Answers to the following questions can help to define SMART goals:

- **S**pecific – What do I want to achieve and why?
- **M**easurable – How will I know I have achieved success?
- **A**chievable – Is it attainable and within my reach?
- **R**elevant – Does this goal relate to my vision and values?
- **T**ime-bound – When do I need to achieve this by?

Make goals smart**ER** by **E**valuating and **R**eviewing consistently and regularly throughout. Reviewing is discussed more fully in Part Five.

An example SMART goal might be:

To comply with my housing tenancy agreement, I will move all of my belongings currently obstructing access to the boiler and radiators in my home to allow safe access and inspection by an engineer on 10 March 2023.

Breaking down the goal and creating a plan of small actionable steps will help to reduce overwhelm, and incremental progress will increase motivation. For example:

To achieve my goal, I will:

- source bags/boxes for the items I want to sort, organise and keep

- identify a safe space where I can move items to that won't cause an obstruction

- gather items together that I am able to let go of now

- reorganise items currently in the 'safe space' to maximise use of the area

- schedule dates with my helper to maximise support time ahead of the deadline.

In addition to creating goals relating to the client's vision and values, I would suggest including one with the specific aim of increasing the client's overall knowledge and understanding of HD or ND; akin to psychoeducation,[1] this could help to better manage the symptoms of the condition(s) going forward. However, usually no more than three or four goals should be set at any one time to ensure they are manageable and achievable. The pace at which a client makes progress is as individual and unique as they are, and it is helpful for their motivation to set short-, mid- and longer-term goals and outcomes.

Even in situations that require imminent intervention, goals can still be set with a harm-reduction focus but will be time-critical based on the type and level of risk involved. Fire and safety issues could probably be resolved while the client remains in the home but removal of hazardous waste and treating water, sanitation, hygiene, mould and dampness issues, or pest and rodent infestations, may require the client to be relocated to temporary accommodation. If managed and communicated well, relocating to temporary accommodation could provide an opportunity to get to know more about the client and establish a collaborative working relationship to help the client develop goals and strategies that can either be implemented in the interim or following a planned return to their home.

---

1 'Psychoeducation' refers to the process of providing education and information to those seeking or receiving help and support from mental health services.

CHAPTER 26

Change Readiness and Self-Efficacy

With the luxury of time, we would consider where the client is in terms of their readiness to make changes, and seek to establish their perceived level of confidence in their ability to make changes in their behaviour and home environment. However, quite often the situation requires us to be pragmatic and deal first with immediate concerns, and then come back to assessing change readiness for the work that is likely to follow. Using the self-report scale illustrated in Figure 26.1: Readiness Ruler (Miller & Rollnick, 2013, p.174) is a useful way to quickly assess where the client is in relation to the Transtheoretical Model (Stages of Change).

FIGURE 26.1: READINESS RULER

'Readiness typically indicates a willingness or openness to engage in a particular process or to adopt a particular behaviour' and is conceptualised as a 'combination of the [client's] perceived importance of the problem and confidence in their [ability] to change' (DiClemente, Schlundt & Gemmell, 2004, p.104).

Confidence and belief in our own ability to control our behaviour, complete tasks and keep motivated in order to achieve our goals is known as self-efficacy, which can differ based on the situation and circumstances. 'Since [Professor Emeritus at Stanford University, Albert] Bandura published his seminal 1977 paper, Self-Efficacy: Toward a Unifying Theory of Behavioural Change, the subject has become one of the most studied topics in psychology' (Cherry, 2023). Bandura identified four ways that self-efficacy is achieved:

1. Mastery experiences (performing a task).

2. Social modelling (witnessing others successfully completing a task).

3. Social persuasion (encouragement to believe in one's skills and capabilities to succeed).

4. Psychological responses (reacting to emotional states in particular situations).

The General Self-Efficacy Scale (GSE) (Schwarzer & Jerusalem, 1995) can be used to gain a sense of a client's perceived self-efficacy. The ten-item self-reporting scale requires the client to respond to each of the following statements by selecting 1 of 4 scoring options:

1 = Not at all true, 2 = Hardly true, 3 = Moderately true, 4 = Exactly true

1. I can always manage to solve difficult problems if I try hard enough.

2. If someone opposes me, I can find the means and ways to get what I want.

3. It is easy for me to stick to my aims and accomplish my goals.

4. I am confident that I could deal efficiently with unexpected events.

5. Thanks to my resourcefulness, I know how to handle unforeseen situations.

6. I can solve most problems if I invest the necessary effort.

7. I can remain calm when facing difficulties because I can rely on my coping abilities.

8. When I am confronted with a problem, I can usually find several solutions.

9. If I am in trouble, I can usually think of a solution.

10. I can usually handle whatever comes my way.

Alternatively, you could ask the client to complete the very widely studied measure of readiness for change for an adult population, known as the

University of Rhode Island Client Change Assessment (URICA) Scale (DiClemente, Schlundt & Gemmell, 2004). The URICA Psychotherapy Version 32-Item Self-Report Scale measures The Transtheoretical Model of Change stages: pre-contemplation, contemplation, action and maintenance, for which there are five possible responses to each of the questions: 1 = Strongly disagree, 2 = Disagree, 3 = Undecided, 4 = Agree, 5 = Strongly agree.

1. As far as I'm concerned, I don't have any problems that need changing.	**1** 2 3 4 5
2. I think I might be ready for some self-improvement.	1 2 3 **4** 5
3. I am doing something about the problems that had been bothering me.	1 2 3 **4** 5
4. It might be worthwhile to work on my problem.	1 2 **3** 4 5
5. As far as I'm concerned, I don't have any problems that need changing.	1 **2** 3 4 5
6. I am not the problem one. It doesn't make sense for me to consider changing.	1 **2** 3 4 5
7. I am finally doing some work on my problem.	1 2 3 4 **5**
8. I have been thinking that I might want to change something about myself.	1 2 3 **4** 5
9. I have been successful in working on my problem but I am not sure I can keep up the effort on my own.	1 2 **3** 4 5
10. At times my problem is difficult, but I am working on it.	1 2 3 4 **5**
11. Trying to change is pretty much a waste of time for me because the problem doesn't have to do with me.	1 **2** 3 4 5
12. I'm hoping that I will be able to understand myself better.	1 2 3 4 **5**
13. I guess I have faults, but there is nothing that I really need to change.	1 **2** 3 4 5
14. I am really working hard to change.	1 2 3 **4** 5
15. I have a problem and I really think I should work on it.	1 2 **3** 4 5
16. I'm not following through with what I had already changed as well as I had hoped, and I want to prevent a relapse of the problem.	1 2 3 **4** 5
17. Even though I am not always successful in changing, I am at least working on my problem.	1 2 3 **4** 5
18. I thought once I had resolved the problem, I would be free of it, but sometimes I still find myself struggling with it.	1 2 3 **4** 5

cont.

19. I wish I had more ideas on how to solve my problem.	1 2 3 **4** 5
20. I have started working on my problem but I would like help.	1 2 3 4 **5**
21. Maybe someone or something will be able to help me.	1 2 3 4 **5**
22. I may need a boost right now to help me maintain the changes I have already made.	1 2 3 4 **5**
23. I may be part of the problem, but I don't think I really am.	1 2 **3** 4 5
24. I hope that someone will have some good advice for me.	**1** 2 3 4 5
25. Anyone can talk about changing. I'm actually doing something about it.	1 2 **3** 4 5
26. All this talk about psychology is boring, why can't people just forget about their problems?	1 2 3 4 **5**
27. I'm struggling to improve myself from having a relapse of my problem.	1 2 **3** 4 5
28. It is frustrating but I feel I might have a recurrence of a problem I thought I had resolved.	1 2 3 **4** 5
29. I have worries, but so does the next person.	1 2 3 **4** 5
30. I am actively working on my problem.	1 2 **3** 4 5
31. I would rather cope with my faults than try to change them.	1 **2** 3 4 5
32. After all I have done to try and change my problem, every now and again it comes back to haunt me.	1 2 3 4 **5**

URICA Scoring

Pre-contemplation (PC)	Contemplation (C)	Action (A)	Maintenance (M)
1. **1**	2. **4**	3. **4**	6. **2**
5. **2**	8. **4**	7. **5**	16. **4**

Results from these measurement tools can help us to identify potential barriers that might prevent change from happening and whether, with help and support, the client can tap into their own resourcefulness to make lasting change as well as an awareness of what might trigger a relapse and how to mitigate against this happening. You can use MI techniques discussed earlier to explore the results further. Listen out for DARN (desire, ability, reason, need) statements that will indicate that the client is still deciding to make a change (pre-contemplation), or CAT (commitment, activation, taking steps) statements indicating that the client is ready to actively plan for change (action). Use OARS (open-ended questions, affirmations, reflections, summarising) to elicit and strengthen any change talk and commitment (contemplation) language that you hear.

CHAPTER 27

Problem-Solving

Since problems are likely to arise during any process of change, one of the ways we can support self-efficacy is by helping clients to develop problem-solving skills. Synonymous with the DESIRE method, before we can solve a problem, we need to understand what's at its root. To do this we can explore possible solutions, consider previous experiences, identify preconceived ideas and then decide on a solution. The following are some examples of solutions-focused questions that you can ask as part of the process:

- What would you like to experience instead of this problem?

- How have you been dealing with the problem until now?

- When did you first notice this was becoming a problem?

- What was different about your daily living before the problem existed?

- Suppose you went to sleep one night, and a miracle happened that solved the problems that led to you being here.

  - What is the first thing you would notice?
  - Would you consider that to be a good thing?
  - What difference would that make, and would you be pleased about it?
  - How would your loved ones notice that you were pleased?
  - How might your loved ones' lives also have improved?

'One of the fundamental human cognitive processes is problem solving; where the brain searches for a solution to a given problem or finds a path to reach a given goal' (Wang & Chiew, 2010, p.81). There are several problem-solving methods that can be used based on the type of problem and whether a person's thinking style is more 'convergent' or 'divergent'.

This concept was introduced in 1956 by psychologist J. P. Guilford, who made a distinction between divergent and convergent thinking in how we approach problem-solving. Convergent thinkers tend to focus on finding one well-defined solution with speed, accuracy and logic and may prefer using methods such as 5 Whys and GROW (see below). Divergent thinkers prefer to generate lots of ideas and find multiple solutions, adopting a non-linear, free-flowing, spontaneous approach, and may prefer brainstorming methods such as rapid ideation, role-storming, and mind-mapping.

5 Whys

Developed in the 1930s by the Japanese founder of Toyota, Sakichi Toyoda, (Toyota Industries Corporation, n.d.) and still used by the organisation today, the 5 Whys method follows a line of enquiry that starts by stating the problem. It's important to remain rational and objective. Start by stating the nature of the problem and then ask why it's a problem. Ask 'why' four more times. The root cause of the problem should become clear in the answer to the fifth 'why', and a countermeasure can be sought to prevent the problem from recurring. For example:

- **Problem:** There is an unpleasant smell in the kitchen.

- **1 Why?** There's refuse on the floor.

- **2 Why?** The bin is full and overflowing.

- **3 Why?** I can't take it to the outside wheelie bin.

- **4 Why?** I share it with my neighbour, but they've moved it closer to their front door so they can get to it more easily.

- **5 Why?** It's not easy for me to get to where it is because I can't get that far *without my walking aid and I can't carry heavy or large bags when I'm using it.* (A root cause)

- **Countermeasure:** Arrange with the local authority to provide another wheelie bin.

GROW

First published in the UK (Whitmore, 1992), GROW, which is an acronym for Goal, Reality, Obstacles (and/or Options) and Way forward (optional

When and Who), have become very popular in the coaching profession as a method for goal-setting and problem-solving. An example applying the same problem statement used in 5 Whys is:

- **Goal** – Remove the unpleasant odour from the kitchen.

- **Reality** – Refuse on the floor because the bin is full and overflowing.

- **Obstacles** – Can't access the outside wheelie bin because it has been moved further away from the house.

- **Options** – Move it halfway between neighbouring homes. Ask a neighbour or support worker to take out the rubbish for me. Get a new one solely for my house that can be right outside.

- **Way forward** – Contact the local authority to order an additional outside wheelie bin.

- **When and Who** – Additional Ws can be added if there is an immediate need or commitment to act. 'My support worker can help me to apply online during their next visit on Tuesday.'

Brainstorming

The key aim of any brainstorming method is to quickly generate ideas for solving a specific problem, critique each idea and then choose a good solution. Brainstorming methods are usually fast and can be fun if you agree there are no 'bad' or 'silly' ideas and want to get creative with your thoughts. Some brainstorming techniques include:

- **Rapid ideation** – Quick fire activity (four to six minutes) followed by a longer assessment exercise (approximately 20 minutes) and a final exercise (approximately five minutes) to select a suitable solution.

- **Role-storming** – Consider the problem from someone else's point of view; put yourself in the shoes of a famous inspirational or historical person. This technique helps to shed inhibitions and consider alternative perspectives.

- **Mind-mapping** – Visual exercise that starts with one central idea and lets thoughts develop organically without concern for structure and uses creative ways (lines, colours, symbols) to connect to sub-ideas that stem from the main idea.

CHAPTER 28

Behaviours and Habits

It's important to note that although a client is willing to engage and start working with a practitioner it does not mean they are ready immediately to change their habits and create new behaviour patterns. 'A habit is an already formed reaction to a situation or answer to a problem. Because it is already formed, it develops a certain inertia and resistance to change' (Maslow, 1970, p.245).

> Habits are automatic behavioural responses to environmental cues, thought to develop through repetition of behaviour in consistent contexts. When habit is strong, deliberate intentions have been shown to have a reduced influence on behaviour. The habit concept may provide a mechanism for establishing new behaviours, and so healthy habit formation is a desired outcome for many interventions. Habits also however represent a potential challenge for changing ingrained unhealthy behaviours, which may be resistant to motivational shifts. (Lally & Gardner, 2013, p.137)

According to James Clear (2018), author of *Atomic Habits*, 'bad habits repeat themselves not because you don't want to change but because you have the wrong system for change'.

Clear believes a framework for building a habit can be divided into four steps: cue, craving, response, and reward:

1. (Cue) Make it obvious

   Write down the current habit you want to change.

2. (Craving) Make it attractive

   Create a motivation ritual by doing something you enjoy immediately before the new potentially challenging habit.

3. (Response) Make it easy

   Create an environment that makes the new habit easier to establish.

4. (Reward) Make it satisfying

Reinforce the new habit with an immediate reward.

As highlighted in Chapter 2, cognitive functions that result in specific behaviours associated with problematic clutter are acquiring and saving, decision-making, memory, categorising and organising (Frost & Hartl, 1996), and perfectionism (Frost *et al.*, 1990), for which there are strategies and techniques that can be used by clients that will help them to become consciously aware of their habits. The sub-sections below highlight specific strategies to address these behaviours individually, as well as strategies for letting go.

Acquiring

Sourcing and acquiring stuff can happen both actively and passively. I once worked with a client whose home was filled mostly with items that had been given to her by other people who she said, 'knew she was a bit of a magpie', which initially she enjoyed but had later become overwhelming, and she felt unable to refuse until she quite literally ran out of space.

An estimated 80–95 per cent (Frost, 2009) of people with HD actively acquire excessively. Using the Measurement of Compulsive Hoarding: Saving Inventory–Revised (Frost *et al.*, 2004) can help a client to assess their saving habits with the aim of changing behaviour, but first let's consider the items a client has already sourced and acquired to identify patterns of behaviour.

In this exercise, inspired by one from Glovinsky (2002, p.23–25), 'things' can be split into two stages and carried out over two separate sessions.

Stage 1: Ask the client to spend about an hour (broken down into chunks of time, or by room if easier) and go round their home with a pad and pencil to write down as many items as possible along with notes about where each item came from, why it was kept, thoughts that spring to mind when they see it, and how they feel about it now. Again, if it's easier for the client, the information can be structured using columns or with a paragraph for each item. For example:

Item	Source	Emotions
Baby elephant	Gift from sister	Favourite in my collection. Pretty fabric. Would not want to part with it.

Or:

> (West) German pottery vase: one of a handful of carefully selected pieces I bought for myself as a reminder of my place of birth. I like the shape and colours; the glaze makes me think of a valley with a river running through and a blue sky above. I would feel sad if I had to let it go.

Stage 2: Working with the client, review the list of items captured and look for common reasons for acquiring and saving that may allude to behaviour patterns such as impulsive, compulsive, sentimental, instrumental, intrinsic, guilt, disorganisation, procrastination, memory. Being able to identify past and present reasons can help to inform future decisions about acquiring and saving habits.

Modified from *Buried in Treasures* (Tolin *et al.*, 2014) and *Treatment for Hoarding Disorder: Workbook* (Steketee & Frost, 2014), the following exercises can help clients to reduce compulsive acquiring habits by learning to develop control over urges to acquire and to remove emotion from the process of acquiring. Again, these exercises can be split into steps for completion by the client and joint evaluation during planned future sessions.

Step 1: Discussing with the client the process of acquiring

The process of acquiring usually begins with a state of emotional vulnerability, followed by a trigger – something seen, heard or experienced that activates thoughts about acquiring. Our thoughts, feelings and beliefs determine what happens next. On acquisition of an item, an immediate emotional payoff (joy, relief, victory) is experienced, and this creates a hook (desire) to repeat the emotional response. Once the 'high' of acquiring wears off (from a few minutes to a few weeks or months afterwards), regret kicks in and shapes our negative self-perceptions and leads to low mood. To combat sadness and frustration we repeat the process again and again.

Ask the client to complete the following exercise to understand their own acquiring process.

Thinking about an item you recorded in the acquiring log – remember back to the time before, during, and after you acquired the item and make a note of the following details, paying particular attention to the first three steps:

Beginning emotional state:

Acquiring trigger:
Thoughts that make acquiring more likely:
Immediate emotional experience after acquiring:
Development of regret:
Negative conclusions about yourself:

Step 2: Helping the client to create strategies to reduce acquiring

Discuss possible strategies for reducing acquiring, since many people who acquire compulsively seem to lose themselves in the moment, becoming 'hyper-focused' and forgetting about everything other than the item in front of them. One strategy that aims to bring everything back into focus and help the client to make a more informed decision about acquiring is to establish a set of rules to follow, for example:

I cannot get this unless:

- I plan to use it within the next week.

- I have enough money right now to pay for it.

- I have a place to put it so it doesn't add to the clutter.

- Acquiring this item is consistent with my goals and values for my life.

- I have a true need, not just a wish, for this item.

Some rules set can be temporary and goal based. For example:

- I will not get any new books until I have read the three set aside.

You can also ask the client to think about and tell you the advantages and disadvantages of acquiring items. For example:

Advantages of buying more books:

- It was reduced so I got a bargain.

- I've got more knowledge at my fingertips.

Disadvantages of buying more books:

- I've got so many other books still to read.

- It took me over my weekly budget.

Step 3: Supporting the client to tolerate triggers to acquire

Triggers to acquire can be anything and will be unique to each and every client. Triggers can provoke powerful urges to acquire that may seem impossible to control, but once a client learns to tolerate the urges, they will become less intense and more controllable. Using an exposure strategy is one way to help a client to gradually expose themselves to triggers to acquire, starting with 'weaker' triggers and building up to 'stronger' more powerful ones.

First, ask the client to list likely triggers, and using a scale of 0 = None to 10 = Significant, rate the level of intensity for each one, or if easier rate the level of discomfort they believe they would feel if the trigger was ignored, and no acquisition made. For example:

Situation	Urge or discomfort level (0 = None – 10 = Significant)
Driving past (favourite superstore)	7
Browsing in my local charity shop	8
Picking up something left on the kerbside	4

Ideally, you would accompany the client to support them as they expose themselves to acquiring triggers and gradually build up their levels of tolerance or reduce their levels of discomfort. Remind the client that they're working hard to change long-standing habits and it will take time and practice to weaken their urges to acquire.

Step 4: Developing rerouting strategies as alternatives to acquiring

As we've already established, changing habits requires us to change our behaviours. We can help clients to identify other pleasurable activities they could participate in either on their own or with others – perhaps by accessing services in their local community. Ideally, the options will include activities that can be done both at home and away from the home. With the client, brainstorm some ideas but be mindful of only adding those activities that appeal to the client. Examples of activities might include:

- join/visit the library
- read (or listen to) a book
- set up your player and listen to music
- attend a local community group
- work on an unfinished project
- call or visit a friend or family member.

Pin the list on a prominent wall in the client's home where they will notice it so it is more likely to prompt them to try out one of the activities.

Saving

As we know from studies (Furby, 1978), we all keep items for sentimental reasons, for their value and usefulness, or because we find them to be aesthetically pleasing, which in and of itself is not problematic. But as is the case for clients with HD or ND, when one or more of these reasons is applied to almost every item kept, and belongings are unorganised or not stored securely, their homes can have limited functional space and become unsafe. Some people are affected by 'disposophobia' which is defined as 'fear of getting rid of stuff'. Disposophobia creates anxiety and can lead to panic attacks and obsessive thoughts, as well as feelings of hopelessness or disconnect.

Turning to the Saving Inventory–Revised (Frost *et al.*, 2004), asking a client to complete this questionnaire will help them to understand their own thoughts about keeping items as well as the impact on their home and daily life.

Clutter subscale

The following questions are answered using the following response choice options:

0 = None, 1 = A little, 2 = A moderate amount, 3 = Most/Much, 4 = Almost all/Complete

1. How much of the living area in your home is cluttered with possessions? (Consider the amount of clutter in your kitchen, living

room, dining room, hallways, bedrooms, bathrooms and other rooms).

2. How much control do you have over your urges to acquire possessions?

3. How much of your home does clutter prevent you from using?

4. How much control do you have over your urges to save possessions?

5. How much of your home is difficult to walk through?

Difficulty discarding/saving subscale

The following questions are answered using the following response choice options:

0 = Not at all, 1 = Mild, 2 = Moderate, 3 = Considerable/Severe, 4 = Extreme

6. To what extent do you have difficulty throwing things away?

7. How distressing do you find the task of throwing things away?

8. To what extent do you have so many things that your room(s) are cluttered?

9. How distressed or uncomfortable would you feel if you could not acquire something you wanted?

10. How much does clutter in your home interfere with your social, work or everyday functioning? Think about things that you don't do because of clutter.

11. How strong is your urge to buy or acquire for free things for which you have no immediate use?

12. To what extent does clutter in your home cause you distress?

13. How strong is your urge to save something you know you may never use?

14. How upset or distressed do you feel about your acquiring habits?

15. To what extent do you feel unable to control the clutter in your home?

16. To what extent has your saving or compulsive buying resulted in financial difficulties for you?

Acquisition subscale

The following questions are answered using the following response choice options:

0 = Never, 1 = A Rarely, 2 = Sometimes/Occasionally, 3 = Frequently/Often, 4 = Never

17. How often do you avoid trying to discard possessions because it is too stressful or time consuming?

18. How often do you feel compelled to acquire something you see? For example, when shopping or offered free things?

19. How often do you decide to keep things you do not need and have little space for?

20. How frequently does clutter in your home prevent you from inviting people to visit?

21. How often do you actually buy (or acquire for free) things for which you have no immediate use or need?

22. To what extent does the clutter in your home prevent you from using parts of your home for their intended purpose? For example, cooking, using furniture, washing dishes, cleaning.

23. How often are you unable to discard a possession you would like to get rid of?

Questionnaire scoring subscales are:

- Clutter subscale (9 items): 1, 3, 5, 8, 10, 12, 15, 20, 22
- Difficulty discarding/saving subscale (7 items): 4, 6, 7, 13, 17, 19, 23
- Acquisition subscale (7 items): 2, 9, 11, 14, 16, 18, 21

Similar to acquiring rules (above), a strategy that could help the client to change their thoughts about saving is to create a set of questions (Tolin et al., 2014, pp.78–79) they can ask themselves when deciding whether to keep or let go of items. For example:

- How many do I already have and is that enough?
- Have I used this in the past year?
- Does this fit with my own values and needs?

- Does this just seem important to me because I am looking at it now?

- Would I buy it again if I didn't already own it?

- Could I get it again if I found I really needed it?

- Do I have enough space for this?

- Will not having this help me to solve my [clutter] problem?

Letting go

I prefer to use the term 'letting go' when talking to a client about their personal possessions because I think it has a more positive connotation than discarding, dumping or getting rid of. In my early years of working alongside people with lived experience of hoarding or chronic disorganisation, I was struck by the unique and ritualistic methods some of them adopted when deciding to let go of an item. For example, while processing thoughts about whether to keep or to let go of a scarf, a client 'spoke' to it and said: 'Thank you, scarf; we've been to some nice places together. You added some colour to my life, but I think it's time to pass you on to someone else.' She then kissed her scarf, said 'Goodbye' and placed it in a bag destined for her local charity shop. Another client was considering whether to let go of a big teddy bear that her ex-partner had given her. She lay down on her bed holding the teddy bear and closed her eyes. I instinctively understood that in doing so she was trying to determine whether it was still a source of comfort to her, but she concluded she no longer felt any emotional connection to the bear, or what it had once represented, so she decided to let it go.

In addition to those early experiences, I have seen many other methods used over the years. While I understand that to some people, these may seem a little unconventional, I would encourage you to embrace and support whatever ritual a client performs that will help them with the process of letting go.

CHAPTER 29

Decision-Making

We make decisions based on our core beliefs and thought processes which are often maladaptive in people with lived experience of HD or ND, but we can use cognitive and behavioural therapy techniques to help clients recognise, examine and change problematic thoughts. Techniques such as *Socratic questioning* can help a client to explore thoughts and beliefs logically and assess their validity. For them to feel able to do this we should aim to create an atmosphere of '"productive discomfort," not panic and intimidation' (Reis, 2003). Socratic questioning was named after Socrates and the teaching method he used for encouraging his students to discover answers by asking questions. Plato, a student of Socrates, wrote:

> The teacher feigns ignorance about a given subject in order to acquire another person's fullest possible knowledge of the topic. Individuals have the capacity to recognize contradictions, so Socrates assumed that incomplete or inaccurate ideas would be corrected during the process of disciplined questioning, and hence would lead to progressively greater truth and accuracy. (SERC, 2023)

Below are example Socratic questions for different situations.

Clarifying thinking
To get the client thinking expressly about their exact thoughts to prove the concepts behind their answer or argument, use basic 'tell me more' questions that get them to go deeper.

Why do you say that?
Could you explain further?
What do you mean by...?
How does this relate to what we have been talking about?
What do we already know about this?

Can you give me an example?
Are you saying...or...?
Can you restate that with a bit more clarity and precision?
How do you feel about this?

Challenging assumptions

To challenge the client's assumptions and make them think about the presuppositions and unquestioned beliefs on which they are founding their answer, ask:

Is this always the case?
What assumptions have you made here?
You seem to be assuming...?
What beliefs might you be basing your argument on?
How can you verify or disprove that assumption?
What exceptions are there to this?
Please explain why/how...?

Using evidence in arguments

When a client gives a rationale for their argument, dig into that reasoning and challenge unthought-through or weakly understood supports for their arguments.

What evidence do you have for this?
Is there reason to doubt this evidence?
How do you know this?
Can you support this with a reasoned argument?
Can you give me an example of that?
Are these reasons good enough?
How might it be refuted?
On what authority are you basing your argument?

Exploring alternative perspectives

Most arguments are given from a particular position, and we can challenge the position to show that there are other, equally valid, viewpoints.

How else could you answer this?
What is the counter-argument?
Who might see this differently? Why?
Another view is.... Does this seem reasonable?
How might a...answer this?
How could...apply here?
What is the difference between...and...?
Why is this...better than...?
What are the strengths and weaknesses of...?

Considering the consequences

The argument the client gives may have logical implications that can be forecast but we can question their sensibility and desirability.

What would happen if...happened?
Then what would happen?
What would happen if everyone did/believed this?
What would happen if you...didn't do this?

Questioning the question

We can be reflexive and turn the question in on itself by using the client's own reasoning and putting the ball back into their court.

What was the point of asking that question?
Why is this question important?
Why do you think I asked this question?
Am I making sense? Why not?
What else might I ask?
What does that mean?
What other questions could I ask?

The Downward Arrow

Another cognitive and behavioural therapy technique we can use, illustrated in Figure 29.1: The Downward Arrow, starts by asking the client to identify a situation or activity that provokes unhelpful thoughts. Then, with the use of Socratic questioning, we can help them to uncover their core beliefs.

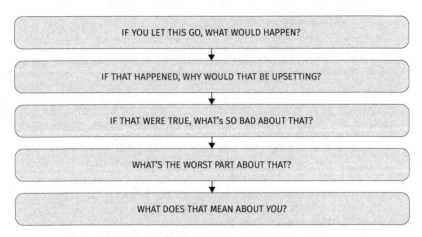

FIGURE 29.1: THE DOWNWARD ARROW

On the final step, when the client has exhausted their thoughts, link their final response to the original fearful situation or activity with the aim of helping the client to understand their assumptions based on distorted thoughts and beliefs.

CHAPTER 30

Procrastination and Perfectionism

Perfectionism and procrastination are characteristically linked. Setting high standards and fear of failure associated with perfectionism can result in avoiding tasks to minimise stress due to not meeting such standards, thus creating a cycle of perfectionism induced procrastination. Research suggests that 15–25 per cent of adults chronically procrastinate, and procrastination can be linked to depression, anxiety, low self-esteem, poor impulse control and ADHD (Ferrari, 2007; Steel, 2007).

We each have our own reasons for procrastinating, for example, feeling overwhelmed or perfectionism and fear of making a mistake, but putting off what we need to do increases our stress levels and prevents us from achieving our goals. Also, if we put something off for too long and end up doing it in a rush, we're more likely to make mistakes, thus acting as a self-fulfilling prophecy.

One of the most common belief patterns of procrastination associated with hoarding behaviour is what's described as 'overcommitted wishful thinking' and is related to setting unrealistic goals as a way to provide a safe escape psychologically in the short term. Beliefs such as 'Because I have too many things to do (or this task is too difficult for me), it's not a big issue that I don't follow through with my goals' may be distressing for the client but can also be frustrating to others, including loved ones who may view it as passive-aggressive behaviour.

One of my favourite quotes is by American professional tennis player Arthur Ashe: 'Start where you are; use what you have; do what you can', which I recount often if I sense a client is feeling overwhelmed or fearful. I suggest we focus on one thing that is right in front of us and take it from there. Sometimes just getting started is the hardest part so keep it small and focused, and reward completion – nothing big, perhaps just a few minutes rest or a cup of tea. If it works for the client, use a timer, and build up to extending the time period for activity and reward.

Other common fears are the unknown, failure, ability, time and choice. To help clients overcome fears and avoidance I use a 3Rs technique adapted from acceptance and commitment therapy (ACT):

1. *Recognise* – acknowledge thoughts and feelings related to avoidance.

2. *Resolve* – identify reasons for avoiding the activity or situation.

3. *Respond* – act based on values and achievement of goals.

Below is an example of how the 3Rs technique can be applied to an established goal.

Goal: To comply with my housing tenancy agreement, I will move all of my belongings currently obstructing access to the boiler and radiators in my home to allow safe access and inspection by an engineer on 10 March 2023.

Action: I will gather items together that I am able to let go of right now.

Activity avoidance thought: I can't gather any items to let go because I need all of them!

1. *Recognise*

   Is that really true or am I trying to avoid doing this because I feel anxious?

2. *Resolve*

   What if I make the wrong decision about what to let go? I'll have failed again.

3. *Respond*

   But I really need to create space so I can get the boiler fixed, so I'll start with finding one thing to let go of that I know I could get again if I really needed to.

The term 'perfectionism' refers less to wanting something to be 'right' or 'perfect' and more to fear of getting something 'wrong'. It is 'the desire to achieve the highest standards of performance, in combination with unduly critical evaluations of one's performance' (Frost & Marten, 1990). Frost and Marten developed a measure (1990; Stober, 1998), named the

Frost Multidimensional Perfectionism Scale (FMPS), designed specifically to assess dimensions of perfectionism in clinical and non-clinical groups. Perfectionism isn't a formal diagnostic category, but it has been associated with multiple forms of psychopathology, including anxiety, depression, eating disorders and suicidality (Egan, Wade & Shafran, 2011; Limburg *et al.*, 2017; Smith *et al.*, 2019). Symptoms of perfectionism include intense fear of failure, harsh self-criticism, use of counterproductive performance-related behaviours, task-avoidance and procrastination. Helpful interventions include addressing common thinking errors by using the cognitive techniques discussed earlier in this book.

Researchers suggest perfectionism may be a 'transdiagnostic process', central to increasing individuals' vulnerability to and maintenance of serious mental health problems and an important predictor of treatment outcome (Egan *et al.*, 2011). A 'transdiagnostic process' is the term used to describe an element of a disorder found in the areas of attention, memory, thinking, reasoning and behaviour. An example of a transdiagnostic processes is repetitive negative thinking, which is a feature of both generalised anxiety disorder and depression.

CHAPTER 31

Developing Strategies and Techniques

Managing stress and anxiety

When working with clients in their home, it is highly likely that at some point they will feel overwhelmed, stressed and anxious. Be prepared to support them through these experiences by adopting evidence-based strategies and techniques. Being able to manage the situation and 'normalising' the client's physical and mental state will instil confidence in you as their helper and influence how they move forward. Clinical psychologist Dr Krystal Lewis (National Institute of Mental Health, 2021) created the acronym GREAT, meaning Gratitude, Relaxation, Exercise, Acknowledge feelings and Track thoughts, as an easy reminder to engage in helpful practices for managing stress and anxiety.

- **Gratitude** – finding small things each day to be grateful about.

- **Relaxation** – techniques to reduce stress and anxiety, such as 'grounding'.

- **Exercise** – being active benefits both our physical and mental health.

- **Acknowledge** – use the 3Rs to recognise, resolve and respond to your feelings.

- **Track** – monitor your thoughts and change any that are distorted.

Grounding techniques

Grounding techniques are scientifically proven coping strategies to help separate the person from the emotional state or situation that is causing distress. They are tools that can be used to help switch off the 'fight or flight' response and 'ground' us in the present moment.

Five Senses

Look around you and identify:

- five things you SEE
- four things you FEEL
- three things you HEAR
- two things you SMELL
- one thing you TASTE.

Mind and body

- Take a long, deep breath in through your nose, and exhale through the mouth. Repeat this two or three times.

- With both feet placed flat on the floor, first wiggle your toes then curl and uncurl your toes. Repeat this a few more times and pay attention to the sensations in your feet.

- Stamp your feet up and down on the ground several times and again, pay attention to the sensations in your legs and feet as they contact with the ground.

- Clench your hands into fists, then release and let go of the tension. Repeat this several times.

- Press your palms together; press them harder and hold for ten seconds. Pay attention to the feeling of tension in your hands and arms.

- Rub your palms together briskly; notice the sound and the sensation.

- Reach your hands above your head and reach towards the sky. Hold this stretch for around five to eight seconds and then bring your arms down and let them relax at your sides.

- Once again, take a few deep breaths in through your nose, exhale through the mouth, and notice the feeling of calmness.

Focus and attention

Clients with lived experience of HD or CD often have difficulty maintaining focus while sorting their belongings; whether this is due to baseline inattentiveness, or the distracting power of emotional activation has not yet been established (Woody *et al.*, 2021). Also, the type of task may have increased ecological validity[1] for the information processing style associated with HD (Grisham *et al.*, 2010).

A general rule of thumb for sorting sessions is to break it down as 'time, target, and task', working in fairly short blocks of time followed by a quick 'time out', focusing on one specific area or activity, and working only on one task at a time. This can help to reduce overwhelm and increase motivation as a client feels a sense of achievement from each activity.

- **Time:** Set a timer or alarm using a watch, clock, mobile phone or sand timer (hourglass), but try to avoid timers with a loud 'tick' as it could be distracting. The time blocks will of course vary depending on the client and the overall length of your session. If I had a two-hour session, I might suggest breaking it down into four half-hour sections: 20 minutes of activity followed by a ten-minute time-out break. The time-out breaks provide a good opportunity to chat with the client and get to know more about them as well as finding out their thoughts and feelings about progress (or lack of) being made.

- **Target:** If targeting by area, keep it small: identify an area within a room such as a doorway, window or in front of a heat source, or find a functional item such as tabletop or sofa. Alternatively, you could target by activity and perhaps aim to gather specific items from every room and bring them back to a central point. Obviously, this option can only be considered if there is enough space to move safely around the client's home but this can be a very helpful method for sorting and categorising items with the aim of helping the decision-making process. I once did this exercise with a client who had a large number of handbags. We brought them all into one room and sorted them by colour, which enabled her to immediately decide to let go of the brown ones

---

1   Ecological validity, in psychology, is defined by Encyclopædia Britannica as 'a measure of how test performance predicts behaviours in real-world settings'.

because she acknowledged that she only ever used blue or black coloured handbags.

- **Task:** Using a timeframe and targeting a specific area or function should help to keep the client focused on individual tasks and completing them one by one. Doing so will provide a sense of achievement and increased motivation to continue. Completing tasks may make the client feel stressed or anxious, so chat with them beforehand about anything that could help them to cope better. Some people might like listening to music or using other sources of 'noise' to help them feel calm. Doctor of Audiology Amy Sarow affirms 'certain colours [of noise] have shown potential benefits within neurodivergent circles and helped with focus. This is because certain hues of sound change the base "state" of the brain' (Lo, 2022). The colour of sound can help 'people with anxiety as they tend to be on high alert...the use of pink or brown noise may reduce their reactivity to those little sounds in their environment and support calming, sleep, or even concentration' (Lo, 2022). Examples of brown noise include thunder, crashing waves, heavy waterfalls. Examples of pink noise include wind blowing through trees, low waves and steady rainfall.

Before we look at a variety of different organising methods taking these challenges into consideration, I'd like to suggest some dos and don'ts:

- Don't underestimate the amount of time tasks and activities can take, especially for clients who are chronically disorganised or have lived experience of ND.

- Don't overcomplicate systems and processes; keep them concise and straightforward.

- Do make sure that any new methods developed are meaningful and intuitively understood by the client.

- Do expect the client to become frustrated or upset when they feel as if their existing systems are being dismantled.

- Do accept that the environment is likely to get worse before it gets better.

Psychiatrist and co-author of *Driven to Distraction* Ned Hallowell (Hallowell & Ratey, 1995, p.177) said, 'In order to arrange life, in order to create, one must get comfortable with disarrangement for a while.' This is true for both client and practitioner: clients with HD/CD/ND are already living with 'disarrangement' and probably have been for many years, albeit not often comfortably, but comfort is subjective. Some practitioners, on the other hand, might find it a little more challenging and as a result, may work at a faster pace than is manageable or tolerable for the client. If we think about clutter as a continuum with order at one end and disorder at the other end, a good place to aim for is somewhere in the middle and trying to find the right balance for the client, which may be different from where other people want them to be. Again, maintaining a focus on health, safety and wellbeing will help bridge the gap between order and disorder, without exerting personal standards or judgements.

Checking in and out

Before tackling the practical tasks during a scheduled sorting and organising session, it's always good to start by checking in with the client by asking them how they're feeling at that moment and how they have been since the previous session: have they coped with any changes made, did they attempt or complete any tasks set, have they experienced any challenges or difficulties? Then, to bring the focus back to the present you could ask, 'What would you like to achieve in the time we have today?', 'What do you hope to gain from our session?', 'What do you feel up to working on today?' or, 'I thought we could maybe work on... What do you think? Or is there something else you would like to work on instead?'

This will reinforce the message that the client has control over the plan and will draw on their own strengths and self-efficacy to achieve their goals – reminding them that in the spirit of MI we are doing this *with* them and not *to* them. However, be mindful of any procrastination and avoidance behaviours. Remind the client that change is often difficult and may increase their stress or anxiety, but they can use their learned coping strategies and techniques, and you are there to support them.

As the session is nearing its end, I recommend wrapping up by summarising what you've been working on, and perhaps suggest the client takes a short break to reflect on or reward an achievement. If you've been moving the client's belongings around the home, remind them where items have 'landed' or what items are leaving with you; make a note of them or take a photo if necessary. Ask them if they are okay and if there is anything they want to discuss or ask before you leave, and then schedule your next session.

More often than not, I ask the client if they would like to hug before I leave. This is a purely personal choice but one I feel completely comfortable with, and only ever do with the client's permission. Therapist Virginia Satir famously said: 'We need 4 hugs a day for survival. We need 8 hugs a day for maintenance. We need 12 hugs a day for growth.' And scientific research (Dreisoerner *et al.*, 2021) shows that receiving hugs is a 'simple and yet potentially powerful means for buffering individuals' resilience against stress'.

When someone hugs us, the stimulation of c-tactile afferents (nerve receptors) in our skin sends signals, via the spinal cord, to the brain's emotion processing networks. This induces a cascade of neurochemical signals, which have proven health benefits. Some of the neurochemicals include the hormone oxytocin, which plays an important role in social bonding, slows down heart rate and reduces stress and anxiety levels. The release of endorphins in the brain's reward pathways supports the immediate feelings of pleasure and wellbeing derived from a hug (McGlone & Walker, 2021). I am always acutely aware of the fact that I might be the only person my client has seen (or sometimes spoken with) for days, weeks or even months. Hugging is a way to communicate emotion via touch. This is my way of letting the client know that I admire their courage, acknowledge the difficult challenges they are facing, empathise with the situation and provide support and kindness. Never has anyone refused a hug; often they tell me how much they appreciate it.

Sorting and organising

Consideration should be given to a client's learning style and whether they are predominantly visual, auditory or kinaesthetic learners. Studies (Institute for Challenging Disorganization, 2012, p.214) show that 40–65 per cent of the population have a visual learning style, making it more prevalent than auditory or kinaesthetic styles. Generally speaking, visual learners want to see how a task is done, auditory learners want to hear the task being explained to them, and kinesthetic learners want to do the task themselves. When working with clients there are some things to look and listen out for and be aware of that can help you to identify their predominant learning style. These are explained below.

Visual learners
CLUES FOR VISUAL LEARNERS

- When describing something to you, do they close their eyes?

- Do you see them covering their eyes when they feel overwhelmed?

- Do you hear them saying phrases like 'I see that you mean', 'I can't visualise that' or 'I'd have to write that down or I'm likely to forget.'

METHODS FOR VISUAL LEARNERS

- Incorporate a variety of images, diagrams and written words.

- Use mind-maps, storyboards, flowcharts, vision boards and so on.

- Use colour and highlight key pieces of information.

CONSIDERATIONS FOR VISUAL LEARNERS

- Visual learners often have a good memory and may use mental mind-maps for placement of belongings in their home. Ask permission before moving items because often those piles of stuff that look chaotic to the untrained eye are carefully constructed in a way that makes sense to the client. Moving items is likely to be disorienting and frustrating for the client.

Auditory learners
CLUES FOR AUDITORY LEARNERS

- Do they like to be outside and 'in tune' with mother nature?

- Do they usually have the radio playing in the background?

- During a conversation, do they tend to talk over you?

METHODS FOR AUDITORY LEARNERS

- Go for a walk to discuss plans and activities.

- When you explain something, ask them to repeat it back to you.

- Use lists for instructions; having a list for routine items creates a rhythmic structure.

CONSIDERATIONS FOR AUDITORY LEARNERS

- Avoid providing information or instructions that require a lot of reading.

- Allow enough time to discuss the information and enable the client to talk about it and repeat it, since hearing themselves talk reinforces their learning and can also stimulate their thought processes to create new ideas.

Kinesthetic learners

CLUES FOR KINESTHETIC LEARNERS

- Do you observe them pacing while talking, or fidgeting while you are talking?

- Do you hear phrases like 'How do you do this?' or 'How do other people do this?'

- Do they get up and move around frequently?

METHODS FOR KINESTHETIC LEARNERS

- Discuss ideas together but let the client set up any new systems or processes.

CONSIDERATIONS FOR KINESTHETIC LEARNERS

- Two key phrases to keep in mind are 'in motion' and 'hands on' because 'doing' and 'being' is how the learning process takes place. Keep the client actively involved in completing tasks that allow them to move around and be active if possible.

Bear in mind these are preferred learning styles and that most people will use all of these at different times in different situations. If while working with a client the primary style doesn't work, then just try the others until you find a way that works.

When working with clients who have lived experience of HD, also consider the concept of small steps. I like the Kaizen philosophy, a method whose origins are in continuous improvement. Kaizen is a combination of two words, *Kai* (change) and *Zen* (good), and was introduced in the 1980s by Masaaki Imai who said, 'Kaizen means improvement. Moreover, it means continuing improvement in personal life, home life, social life, and working life' (Kaizen™ Institute, n.d.). It is a way of working that empowers clients to take small steps and make small changes to get significant and lasting results. The science behind Kaizen is that by doing 'little and often' we can bypass the part of our brain (amygdala) that creates the 'fight or flight' response to create new connections that help us form new habits. Even tasks that may seem trivial will, once completed, create a sense of achievement and lead to change both mentally and physically.

However, when working with CD/ND clients, also be mindful of the fact that they may prefer to consider 'the big picture' and deal with it as a whole rather than little pieces of the picture. For some, too many pieces or tasks can be overwhelming and demotivating. Which is why, I'm sure, you're now fully appreciating the need to treat every individual and their situation as unique and apply the most relevant techniques and approaches.

In adopting an Arthur Ashe mindset of 'start where you are, use what you have, do what you can' and, if appropriate, doing it the Kaizen way of 'small steps', some of the techniques listed below may help you and your client to get started and make continuous progress towards sustainable change.

- People with lived experience of HD/CD/ND are often guided by their emotions, not logic, and have a more personalised relationship with their belongings. By rephrasing questions from 'Do you need this?' to 'Does this need you?' the client is more likely to let the item go. Try it! I think you'll be surprised at the response you get.

- Try these random ideas too. Think of them as concepts that you can tweak if necessary to make sure they are 'fit for purpose' and relate specifically to your client and their situation.

    - **Focus:** Reduce overwhelm by adopting a novel approach: using something like a cardboard tube, ask the client to look through and whatever object comes into view is the starting point.

    - **Voicing:** Where possible, ask the client to use their smartphone (or other voice recorder) to record themselves repeating instructions or information provided by you. This will help with any cognitive impairments or information processing.

    - **Landing spot:** Find the most obvious place (for the client) in the home – possibly close to the front door – and create a space to put keys, purse/wallet, mobile phone.

- **Mantra:** In a similar vein to the 'landing spot', before I leave the house, I mutter a mantra 'keys, phone, money', which during Covid became 'keys, phone, money, mask'. This is a simple technique that can be used as a reminder of all the things you need to take with you wherever you go.

- **Errands:** Put a box/basket near the front door where items can be placed that need to leave the home, such as mail to be posted, dry cleaning, things for repair.

- **Processing:** Place a box/basket/folder in a place where the client is most likely to open and process mail; ideally close to where the paper recycling is located, such as a worktop in the kitchen/utility room.

- **Actions:** Create a separate 'to-do' list for daily, weekly and monthly tasks and start each list item with a verb: buy, pay, send, go.

- **Reminders:** Where possible, use technology to set reminders for urgent and important actions; help the client to set an alarm on a mobile phone, or create a 'note to self' email set to send on a specific date and time.

- **Get real time:** For clients who find it challenging to manage their time accurately, ask them to keep a record of activities and log start and finish times to help them manage their time better, based on concrete rather than abstract information.

- **Snapshots:** Taking photos can serve several different purposes. You can use photos as a way of measuring progress, or as a reminder of where things were, how a room was configured. Photos can also be a way to capture and save a memory of an item rather than keep the physical object. Alternatively, take photos of rooms in the client's home and then while away from the home discuss how they feel when they see their home in this two-dimensional way.

- **Stabiliser:** If you consider setting 'homework' tasks, bear in mind that many clients won't feel able to complete tasks without the support and stability of another person to help them remain focused. I think of this as like a child learning to ride a bike who needs the support of stabilisers until they have developed enough confidence in their ability and can then remove them.

- **Look but don't touch:** Some clients have 'tactile sympathy' (Kolberg, 2008, p.32), which means if they touch something they emotionally engage with it and will then feel unable to let it go. Try sorting with you holding the items rather than the client, who can then focus on deciding.

- **Unconventional naming conventions:** Instead of using logical labels for things like filing systems, name them something that is meaningful to the client and that reflects their way of thinking and how they express their thoughts. For example, instead of using 'Utility bills' it might be more reflective of their language to use 'Things I need to keep the lights on and be warm'. When you start working with a client, ask them to speak their thoughts when completing activities so you can tune in to their language and terminology.

- **Treasures (not trash):** Instead of asking a client to gather stuff that might be considered as 'trash', ask them to locate their most treasured possessions. Look for the positives as opposed to the negatives.

- **Folk groups:** When you are sorting groups of items such as plastic tubs, clothes, books, bags and so on, it's useful to have a way of categorising them, for example using the concept of 'Friends, Strangers and Acquaintances' method: friends you want to keep, strangers you rarely if ever meet so you can let them go, acquaintances come and go, suggesting that they can be let go of and sourced again later if really needed.

- **Boxed sets:** Let's be honest, we all like a box or three, don't we!? Sometimes their mere size, shape, material or colour is enough but depending on the items or intended activity, there are many possible arrangements. For example, one 'set' that could be used for sorting items is 'keep, donate, discard, ripen'. 'Ripen' items are ones the client is indecisive about and any items that are put aside to ripen are given a 'use by' date as a way to avoid procrastination. Another set that could be used for organising is 'put away, give away, throw away, transport'. 'Transport' items are ones that don't belong in the room you are working in and need to be transported to a different place in the home.

- **Themes:** Again, many different themes can be used to sort and organise depending on the client and activity, but a couple of suggestions are using a timeline to sort paperwork into 'past, present, future', or bigger-scale categorising using a shopping centre concept, with each room as a different type of store, for example DIY, Homeware, Arts and Crafts, Clothing and Accessories.

- **Hooks:** Help to build a new habit by hooking it onto an already established one; for example, while brushing your teeth before bedtime, practise a gratitude exercise to support wellbeing and promote restful sleep.

In essence, flexibility and creativity are key. Make it fun by letting your imagination run free and tapping into your client's cleverness. One of my favourite things about this job is getting to work with so many wonderfully creative people and discovering all sorts of novel ideas and potential uses for items.

Courageous conversations

Occasionally, a session can become frayed around the edges, especially if emotions are running high and you're working to a tight schedule. For example, the client may feel that changes are being made too quickly, you may feel that the client is procrastinating and avoiding making decisions about letting go, and you haven't yet cleared enough space to allow access for the gas engineer to inspect the boiler the following day.

Stop, take a deep breath, maybe take a short break, and prepare yourself for a conversation about what needs to happen next. Sometimes challenging conversations are necessary to ensure that goals and outcomes are achieved. Use the following as a guide to focus on what needs to be discussed:

- Define what it is you must do to achieve the desired outcomes. Be clear about what needs to happen.

- Start with facts, and then share how you are feeling. It's easier to start with logical facts and sharing our feelings helps to position why the conversation is important to us. Then ask the client to share their facts and feelings to encourage a balanced dialogue.

- Listen without judgement, to show the client how important their views are and that you value the opportunity to have the conversation. In doing so, we can hear things that we aren't aware of and may connect more closely with the client, making them feel valued and respected.

- Be aware of and control any emotional responses. The key to conducting a courageous conversation is being able to identify if a client is slipping into emotional responses (fight or flight). Being able to maintain control over our and others' emotions will keep us on track to achieve our aim.

- Adopt a benevolent mindset and heart-set. This will make all the difference when having a difficult or challenging conversation.

Part Five

REVIEW AND ESTABLISH ONGOING SUPPORT AND MAINTENANCE

LEARNING OBJECTIVE

Following consideration of the value and benefit in evaluating progress as well as relapse prevention, it is expected the reader will be able to support the client to develop strategies to sustain habit-change.

CHAPTER 32

Review and Evaluate

At times, this stage in the process is either forgotten or disregarded, which is regrettable because reviewing and evaluating habit-changes, benefits, learning or other factors that result from the intervention can provide valuable insight for the client and everyone else involved in the planning and implementation stages. And who would want to miss a chance to celebrate success and an opportunity to learn, develop and continuously improve!?

It doesn't have to be a laborious exercise and is generally considered good practice to continuously monitor and evaluate your work with a client and make any necessary refinements along the way, but specifically as your scope of work is nearing completion, it is prudent to formally review progress.

A formal review to evaluate intervention outcomes established during the planning stages should ideally include the client, related profession-als, any ongoing support team members and, if appropriate, friends or family members. Outcomes can be categorised as primary and secondary; primary being the key objective of the intervention, and secondary the impact or effects as a result. For example:

- **Primary outcome** – remove the risk of eviction and potential homelessness due to a breach in the client's tenancy agreement.

- **Secondary outcomes** – enhance the client's quality of life by erad-icating rodent infestation, removal of refuse from the home, create access to ingress and egress, and organise and reduce belongings to minimise fire and safety risks and issues.

Similarly, a modified harm-reduction plan includes what are described as 'hard' outcomes, and often more emphasis is placed on these since they can be more easily quantified. Hard outcomes are usually linked directly to an intervention outcome and are often time-bound; for example, specific actions to avoid risk of eviction, resolve public health issues or enable hospital discharge. 'Soft' outcomes, which are equally important, include factors such as engagement with practitioners and other service providers or healthcare professionals, increased confidence in self-efficacy, skills development, self-determination and improved health, safety and wellbeing. To demonstrate, in a social impact assessment carried out by Life-Pod, clients used the following words to express how they felt both before and after working with us:

- Before: anxious, disgusted, mistrust, isolated, ashamed, embarrassed, demotivated, no visitors [allowed in their home] and slept a lot.

- After: happy, safe, pleased to see us, helpful, change is sustainable, life-changing, spirits lifted, inspired, motivated, energised and miss us when not there.

Additional information can be gathered as part of any review process by asking questions such as:

- What changes have taken place?

- Are the changes made sustainable?

- What have you done that's made a difference?

- Are there any outstanding activities that need to be achieved?

- What, if anything, could you have done differently?

- Are you concerned about any outstanding issues?

- Are you concerned about any risks or issues recurring?

- What plans are in place to mitigate any potential risks or issues?

- Is there a support network in place for the client?

- Is the client happy with the changes made and plans for going forward?

As well as Life-Pod practitioners having a unique approach to the way we work, we provide a consistent client–practitioner relationship. The practitioner who helps the client to define their goals and intervention outcomes is the same one who provides help and support to achieve them. I believe this element of our service delivery aids the development of a strong working relationship, and crucially for the client means they won't encounter the same level of anxiety each time someone new comes into their home, and they don't have to keep repeating personal information and experiences with different helpers. Dependable practitioners whom clients can rely on help to build trust and facilitate improved or renewed relationships with loved ones, the wider community, or other people they may want to connect with.

CHAPTER 33

Maintenance and Support

Having worked hard to make positive habit-change, our role now is to help the client with maintenance and relapse prevention by ensuring strategies and techniques are established to support continued change, either independently or with support from others. The aim of relapse prevention is to identify situations, experiences or opportunities which could make the client susceptible to initial lapses, and to adopt coping strategies to prevent future relapse.

Generally described as a breakdown or setback in an attempt to change of modify behaviour, relapse is a return to previous habits as a response to stressors or stimuli or in relation to symptoms of a comorbid health condition. Having a relapse prevention plan will help to identify such situations in which the client may be vulnerable to relapse and will enable them to employ cognitive and behavioural coping strategies to prevent future relapses in similar situations. For example:

- rerouting plans (see Chapter 28) – identify and employ activities to avoid old acquiring habits

- managing avoidance and procrastination (see Chapter 30) – practise the 3Rs technique to recognise, resolve and respond to intrusive thoughts

- habit tracking (see Chapter 28) – regular use of tools such as charts to monitor progress

- relaxation techniques (see Chapter 31) – practise grounding and gratitude exercises to reduce stress and anxiety.

It is important to highlight that both lapse and relapse are normal and expected stages of the change process and can be overcome. It is not a sign of failure but an indication that the plan perhaps needs some modification to replace older coping strategies with new ones. Also, keep in mind that HD/CD/ND are chronic conditions, therefore our approach is to effect continual progress as opposed to trying to find a 'cure'.

Finally, when your time working with a client ends, try to ensure that they have all the resources necessary for their continued success. And if they go on to receive help from another service provider, seek to complete a phased handover to aid the transition process for the client.

Many of the tools and techniques I have referred to throughout this resource can be downloaded and reused as part of your practice to help people with lived experience of HD and/or CD. You can access them by visiting hoarding.academy/resources.

Afterword

In my endeavour to share my knowledge and experience in helping people affected by problematic clutter, I have augmented my own learning and strengthened my resolve to improve treatment interventions for those with lived experience of hoarding disorder or chronic disorganisation in need of help and support.

When I set off on my 'planning and organising' journey over a decade ago, I would have valued a resource like this one to guide my practice, so I genuinely hope this book, which I think is unique in this field – a *guidebook* written by a specialist practitioner for fellow practitioners and related professionals – is useful and informative. My aim is to steer your journey in the right direction and signpost some interesting junctures along the way, some longer and more challenging than others. However, as merely the chaperon, yours is the most important role as 'the helper' and how you undertake that role is critical to how and when you and your client will reach the desired destination.

To reiterate my viewpoint stated in the Introduction, there is no 'one size fits all' but there is evidence to show that a combination of cognitive and behavioural strategies, motivational interviewing techniques, and development of skills to facilitate and enhance sorting, organising and letting go, when applied with a harm-reduction attitude, can lead to maintainable change and an improvement in a client's health, safety and wellbeing.

As humans, we are complex creatures confronted with cognitive biases and heuristics. Our humanity depends on the help of others, and our default position for providing help should be set to 'with compassion and without judgement'. I am sometimes accused of being 'too soft' or 'too accommodating' but there are far worse things one could be accused of. My point, though, is that when I talk about *people* being kind and compassionate, I don't exclude those with lived experience of HD/ND/CD; they too must sympathise with their family, friends, neighbours and other people affected by their situation. They are far more likely to want to change the situation if they know that in seeking help they will be treated with kindness and respect. Ultimately, we can each contribute to a self-fulfilling prophecy of *with compassion and without judgement*.

Be curious. Be kind.

Yours aye
Linda

Figures and Tables

Figures

Tables

References

Abreu, L. M. & Marques, J. G. (2022). Noah syndrome: A review regarding animal hoarding with squalor. *Innovations in Clinical Neuroscience*, 19(7–9), 48–54.

ACMD. (1988). *Aids and Drugs Misuse: ACMD Report*. London: UK Parliament. Retrieved from https://hansard.parliament.uk/Lords/1988-03-29/debates/9fcfaced-d1af-4eff-aa65-477ccof10fba/AidsAndDrugsMisuseAcmdReport.

Adams, J. & White, M. (2004). Why don't stage-based activity promotion interventions work? *Health Education Research*, 20(2), 237–243. doi: https://doi.org/10.1093/her/cyg105.

Ainsworth, M. D. & Bell, S. M. (1970). Attachment, exploration, and separation: Illustrated by the behaviour of one-year-olds in a strange situation. *Child Development*, 41(1), 49–67. doi: https://doi.org/10.2307/1127388.

Archer, C. A., Kyara, M., Garza, K. & Zakrzewski, J. J. (2019). Relationship between symptom severity, psychiatric comorbidity, social/occupational impairment, and suicidality in hoarding disorder. *Journal of Obsessive-Compulsive and Related Disorders*, 21, 158–164. doi: https://doi.org/10.1016/j.jocrd.2018.11.001.

Amrhein, P. C., Miller, W. R., Yahne, C. E., Palmer, M. & Fulcher, L. (2003). Client commitment language during motivational interviewing predicts drug use outcomes. *Journal of Consulting and Clinical Psychology*, 71, 862–878. doi: 10.1037/0022-006X.71.5.862.

Banerjee, D. (2020). The other side of COVID-19: Impact on obsessive compulsive disorder (OCD) and hoarding. *Psychiatry Research*, 228. doi: https://doi.org/10.1016/j.psychres.2020.112966.

Baron, S. & Stanley, T. (2019). *Strengths-Based Approach: Practice Framework and Practice Handbook*. London: Department of Health and Social Care.

Beck, A. T., Rush, J., Shaw, B. & Emery, G. (1979). *Cognitive Therapy of Depression*. New York, NY: Guilford Press.

Belk, R. W. (1988). Possessions and the extended self. *Journal of Consumer Research*, 15(2), 139–168. www.jstor.org/stable/2489522.

Bleuler, E. (1950[1911]). *Dementia Praecox or the Group of Schizophrenias*. Translated by J. Zinkin. New York, NY: International Universities Press.

Bonnie, E. (2013). How autism became autism: The radical transformation of a central concept of child development in Britain. *History of the Human Sciences*, 26(3), 3–31. doi: 10.1177/0952695113484320.

Boyd, J. E., Otilingam, P. G. & DeForge, B. R. (2014). Brief version of the Internalized Stigma of Mental Illness (ISMI) scale: Psychometric properties and relationship to depression, self esteem, recovery orientation, empowerment, and perceived devaluation and discrimination. *Psychiatric Rehabilitation Journal*, 37(1), 17–23. doi: https://doi.org/10.1037/prj0000035.

Bratiotis, C., Muroff, J. & Lin, N. (2021). Hoarding disorder: Development in conceptualization, intervention, and evaluation. *Focus*, 19(4), 392–404. doi: https://doi.org/10.1176/appi.focus.20210016.

Bratiotis, C., Schmalisch, C. & Steketee, G. (2011). *The Hoarding Handbook*. New York, NY: Oxford University Press.

Bratiotis, C., Woody, S. & Lauster, N. (2019). Coordinated community-based hoarding interventions: Evidence of case management practices. *Families in Society: Journal of Contemporary Social Services*, 100(1), 93–105. doi: https://doi.org/10.1177/1044389418802450.

Braye, S., Orr, D. O. & Preston-Shoot, M. (2011). *Self-Neglect and Adult Safeguarding*. SCIE, Adult's Services. London: Social Care Institute for Excellence. Retrieved from https://www.scie.org.uk/app/uploads/2024/06/self-neglect_general_briefing.pdf.

Brehm, J. W. (1966). *A Theory of Psychological Reactance*. New York, NY: Academic Press.

Brown, D. (2010). *The Lost Symbol* (illustrated edition). London: Bantam Press.

Brug, J. (2004). The Transtheoretical Model and stages of change: a critique: Observations by five Commentators on the paper by Adams, J. and White, M. (2004) Why don't stage-based activity promotion interventions work? *Health Education Research*, 18(6), 664–677. doi: https://doi.org/10.1093/her/cyh005.

Busz, M., Schiffer, K., Voets, A. & Pomfret, A. (2024). Reframing Dutch drug policies: a new era for harm reduction. *Harm Reduction Journal*, 21, 163. doi: https://doi.org/10.1186/s12954-024-01071-1.

Cath, D. C., Nizar, K., Boomsma, D. & Mathews, C. A. (2017). Age-specific prevalence of hoarding and obsessive compulsive. *American Journal of Geriatric Psychiatry*, 25(3), 245–255. doi: https://doi.org/10.1016/j.jagp.2016.11.006.

Chasson, G. S., Hamilton, C. E., Luxon, A. M., De Leonardis, A. J., Bates, S. & Jagannathan, N. (2020). Rendering promise: Enhancing motivation for change in hoarding disorder using virtual reality. *Journal of Obsessive-Compulsive and Related Disorders*, 25. doi: https://doi.org/10.1016/j.jocrd.2020.100519.

Chen, W., McDonald, S., Wearne, T., Sabel, I., Long, E. V. & Grisham, J. R. (2023). A pilot study of adapted social cognition and intervention training (SCIT) for hoarding disorder. *Journal of Obsessive-Compulsive and Related Disorders*, 36, 100776. Retrieved from www.sciencedirect.com/science/article/abs/pii/S2211364922000690.

Cherry, K. (2023, February 27). Self efficacy and why believing in yourself matters. VeryWellMind. Retrieved from www.verywellmind.com/what-is-self-efficacy-2795954.

Chou, C.-Y., Tsoh, J., Vigil, O., Bain, D. *et al.* (2018, April). Contributions of self-criticism and shame to hoarding. *Psychiatry Research*, 242, 488–493. doi: 10.1016/j.psychres.2017.09.030.

Claes, L., Müller, A. & Luyckx, K. (2016). Compulsive buying and hoarding as identity substitutes: The role of materialistic value endorsement and depression. *Comprehensive Psychiatry, 68,* 65–71. doi: https://doi.org/10.1016/j.comppsych.2016.04.005.

Clark, A., Mankikar, G. & Gray, I. (1975). Diogenes syndrome: A clinical study of gross neglect in old age. *The Lancet, 305*(7903). doi: https://doi.org/10.1016/S0140-6736(75)91280-5.

Clark, D. & Beck, A. T. (2010). Cognitive theory and therapy of anxiety and depression: A convergence with neurobiological findings. *Trends in Cognitive Science, 14*(9), 418–424. doi: https://doi.org/10.1016/j.tics.2010.06.007.

Clear, J. (2018). *Atomic Habits.* New York, NY: Avery. https://jamesclear.com/atomic-habits-summary.

Cooke, J. (2017). *Understanding Hoarding.* London: Sheldon Press.

Couchman, W. (1995). Joint education for mental health teams. *Nursing Standard, 10*(7), 32–34.

Department of Health and Social Security (1990). *National Health Service and Community Care Act 1990.* Retrieved from www.legislation.gov.uk/ukpga/1990/19/contents.

DiClemente, C. C., Schlundt, D. & Gemmell, L. (2004). Readiness and stages of change in addiction treatment. *American Journal on Addictions, 13,* 103–119. doi: 10.1080/10550490490435777.

DiClemente, C. C. & Velasquez, M. M. (2002). Motivational Interviewing and the Stages of Change. In W. R. Miller & S. Rollnick (eds), *Motivational Interviewing: Preparing People for Change* (second edition) (pp.201–216). New York, NY: Guilford Press.

Doran, G. T. (1981). There's a S.M.A.R.T. way to write management's goals and objectives. *Management Review, 70,* 35–36.

Dozier, M. E. & Ayers, C. R. (2017). The etiology of hoarding disorder: A review. *Psychopathology, 50*(5), 291–296. doi: https://doi.org/10.1159/000479235.

Dozier, M. E., Bratiotis, C., Broadnax, D. & Le, J. A. (2019). A description of 17 animal hoarding case files from animal control and a humane society. *Psychiatry Research, 272,* 365–368. doi: https://doi.org/10.1016/j.psychres.2018.12.127.

Dozier, M. E., Porter, B. & Ayers, C. R. (2016). Age of onset and progression of hoarding symptoms in older adults with hoarding disorder. *Aging and Mental Health, 20*(7), 736–742. doi: https://doi.org/10.1080/13607863.2015.1033684.

Dozier, M., Speed, K., Davidson, E., Bolstad, C., Nadorff, M. & Ayers, C. (2021). The association between sleep and late life hoarding. *International Journal of Aging and Human Development, 93*(4), 931–942. doi: https://doi.org/10.1177/0091415020974618.

Dreisoerner, A., Junker, N. M., Schlotz, W. , Heimrich, J. *et al.* (2021, October 8). Self-soothing touch and being hugged reduce cortisol responses to stress: A randomized controlled trial on stress, physical touch, and social identity. *Comprehensive Psychoneuroendocrinology, 8.* doi: https://doi.org/10.1016/j.cpnec.2021.100091.

Drury, H., Ajmi, S., Fernández de la Cruz, L., Nordsletten, A. E. & Mataix-Cols, D. (2014). Caregiver burden, family accommodation, health, and well-being in relatives of individuals with hoarding disorder. *Journal of Affective Disorders, 159,* 7–14. doi: https://doi.org/10.1016/j.jad.2014.01.023.

Egan, S. J., Wade, T. D. & Shafran, R. (2011). Perfectionism as a trandiagnostic process: A clinical review. *Clinical Psychology Review*, 203–212. doi: https://doi.org/10.1016/j.cpr.2010.04.009.

Eisenberg, L. (1977). Disease and illness. Distinctions between professional and popular ideas of sickness. Culture, medicine and psychiatry. *Culture, Medicine and Psychiatry*, 1(1), 9–23. doi: https://doi.org/10.1007/BF00114808.

Engel, G. L. (1977). The Need for a New Medical Model: A Challenge for Biomedicine. *Science*, 196, 129–136. doi: 10.1126/science.847460.

Fairfax County. (2023). Fairfax County's Hoarding Strategies: A Governmental Approach. Retrieved from Department Resources: www.fairfaxcounty.gov/code/hoarding/strategies-a-governmental-approach.

Fay, L. (2024). *Conversation Starter*. Retrieved from https://hoarding.academy/resources.

Ferrari, J. R. (2007). Frequent behavioural delay tendencies by adults: International prevalence rates of chronic procrastination. *Journal of Cross-Cultural Psychology*, 38(4), 458–464. doi: https://doi.org/10.1177/0022022107302314.

Festinger, L. (1957). *A Theory of Cognitive Dissonance*. Stanford, CA: Stanford University Press.

Fontenelle, L. F., Muhlbauer, J. E., Albertella, L. & Eppingstall, J (2021). The impact of coronavirus on individuals with problematic hoarding behaviours. *Journal of Psychiatric Research*, 144, 405–411. doi: https://doi.org/10.1016/j.jpsychires.2021.10.042.

Freeman, T. (2014, May 14). Hopes for task force on hoarding. Retrieved from Holyrood: www.holyrood.com/news/view,hopes-for-task-force-on-hoarding_13879.htm.

Frost, T. S. (2009). Excessive acquisition in hoarding. *Journal of Anxiety Disorders*, 23(5), 632–639. doi: 10.1016/j.janxdis.2009.01.013.

Frost, R. O. (2011). When collecting becomes hoarding. *New York Times*. Retrieved from www.nytimes.com/roomfordebate/2011/12/29/why-we-collect-stuff/when-collecting-becomes-hoarding.

Frost, R. O. & Gross, R. C. (1993). The hoarding of possessions. *Behaviour Research and Therapy*, 31(4), 367–381. doi: https://doi.org/10.1016/0005-7967(93)90094-B.

Frost, R. O. & Hartl, T. L. (1996). A cognitive-behavioral model of compulsive hoarding. *Behaviour Research and Therapy*, 34(4), 341–350. doi: https://doi.org/10.1016/0005-7967(95)00071-2.

Frost, R. O., Hartl, T. L., Christian, R. & Williams, N. (1995). The value of possessions in compulsive hoarding: Patterns of use and attachment. *Behaviour Research and Therapy*, 33(8), 897–902. doi: https://doi.org/10.1016/0005-7967(95)00043-W.

Frost, R. O. & Hristova, V. (2011). Assessment of hoarding. *Journal of Clinical Psychology*, 67(5), 456–466. doi: https://doi.org/10.1002/jclp.20790.

Frost, R. O., Kim, H. J., Morris, C., Murray-Close, M. & Steketee, G. (1998). Hoarding, compulsive buying and reasons for saving. *Behaviour Research and Therapy*, 36(7–8), 657–664. doi: https://doi.org/10.1016/S0005-7967(98)00056-4.

Frost, R. O. & Marten, P. A. (1990). Frost Multidimensional Perfectionism Scale (FMPS). Retrieved from NovoPsych: https://novopsych.com.au/assessments/formulation/frost-multidimensional-perfectionism-scale-fmps.

Frost, R. O., Marten, P., Lahart, C. & Rosenblate, R. (1990). The dimensions of perfectionism. *Cognitive Therapy and Research*, 449–468. doi: https://doi.org/10.1007/BF01172967.

Frost, R. O., Steketee, G. & Williams, L. (2000, July). Hoarding: A community health problem. *Health and Social Care in the Community*, 8(4), 229–234. doi: 10.1046/j.1365-2524.2000.00245.x.

Furby, L. (1978). Possession in humans: An exploratory study of its meaning and motivation. *Social Behavior and Personality: An International Journal*, 6(1), 49–65. https://doi.org/10.2224/sbp.1978.6.1.49.

Gibb, C. E., Morrow, M., Clarke, C., Cook, G., Gertig, P. & Ramprogus, V. (2009). Transdisciplinary working: Evaluating the development of health and social care provision in mental health. *Journal of Mental Health*, 11(3), 339–350. doi: https://doi.org/10.1080/09638230020023714.

Gibson, A. K., Rasmussen, J., Steketee, G., Frost, R. & Tolin, D. (2010). Ethical considerations in the treatment of compulsive hoarding. *Cognitive and Behavioural Practice*, 426–438. doi: https://doi.org/10.1016/j.cbpra.2009.06.008.

Gledhill, L. J., Bream, V., Drury, H. & Onwumere, J. (2021). Information processing in hoarding disorder: A systematic review of the evidence. *Journal of Affective Disorders Reports*, 3, 100039. doi: https://doi.org/10.1016/j.jadr.2020.100039.

Glovinsky, C. (2002). *Making Peace with the Things in Your Life: Why Your Papers, Books, Clothes, and Other Possessions Keep Overwhelming You and What to Do About It*. New York, NY: St Martin's Press.

Goldfarb, Y. Z. (2021). Autistic adults' subjective experiences of hoarding and self-injurious behaviors. *Autism*, 25(5), 1457–1468. doi: https://doi.org/10.1177/1362361321992640.

Gordon, T. (1970). *Parent Effectiveness Training: The Nolose Program for Raising Responsible Children*. New York, NY: Wyden.

Gordon Training International. (n.d.) The Roadblocks to Communication. Retrieved from www.gordonmodel.com/work-roadblocks.php.

Gov.uk. (2013, February 27). Equality Act 2010: Guidance. Retrieved from Government UK: www.gov.uk/guidance/equality-act-2010-guidance.

Green, A. R., Carrillo, J. E. & Betancourt, J. R. (2002). Why the disease-based model of medicine fails our patients. *Western Journal of Medicine*, 176(2), 141–143.

Grisham, J. R. (2006). Age of onset of compulsive hoarding. *Journal of Anxiety Disorders*, 20(5), 675–686.

Grisham, J. R., Martyn, C., Kerin, F. Peter A. *et al.* (2018). Interpersonal functioning in Hoarding Disorder: An examination of attachment styles and emotion regulation in response to interpersonal stress. *Journal of Obsessive-Compulsive and Related Disorders, 16*, 43–49. doi: https://doi.org/10.1016/j.jocrd.2017.12.001.

Grisham, J. R., Norberg, M. M., Williams, A. D., Certoma, S. P. & Kadib, R. (2010). Categorization and cognitive deficits in compulsive hoarding. *Behaviour Research and Therapy*, 48(9), 866–872. https://doi.org/10.1016/j.brat.2010.05.011.

Guilford, J. P. (1956). The structure of intellect. *Psychological Bulletin*, 53, 267–293. doi: https://doi.org/10.1037/h0040755.

Hagger, M. S., Cameron, L. D., Hamilton, K. & Hankonen, N. (eds) (2020). *The Handbook of Behaviour Change*. Cambridge: Cambridge University Press.

Hall, K. (2012). Motivational interviewing techniques: Facilitating behaviour change in the general practice setting. *Australian Family Physician*, 41(9), 660–667. Retrieved from www.racgp.org.au/afp/2012/september/motivational-interviewing-techniques.

Hallowell, N. & Ratey, J. J. (1995). *Driven to Distraction: Recognizing and Coping with Attention Deficit Disorder from Childhood through Adulthood*. New York, NY: Touchstone.

Hartl, T. L., Duffany, S. R., Allen, G. J., Gail, S. & Frost, R. O. (2005). Relationships among compulsive hoarding, trauma, and attention-deficit/hyperactivity disorder. *Behaviour Research and Therapy*, 43(2), 269–276. doi: https://doi.org/10.1016/j.brat.2004.02.002.

Hoarding of Animals Research Consortium (HARC). (2002). Health implications of animal hoarding. *Health and Social Work*, 27(2), 125–136, doi: https://doi.org/10.1093/hsw/27.2.125.

Holmes, S., Whomsley, S. & Kellett, S. (2015, April 1). *A Psychological Perspective on Hoarding*. Leicester: British Psychological Society. Retrieved from British Psychological Society: https://explore.bps.org.uk/content/report-guideline/bpsrep.2024.inf240b.

Institute for Challenging Disorganization. (2011). Clutter–Hoarding Scale®: A Residential Observational Tool. Retrieved from https://www.challengingdisorganization.org/assets/ICDPublications/C-HS/ICD%C2%AE%20C-HS%C2%AE%202021%20Full%20Version.pdf

Institute for Challenging Disorganization. (2012). *The ICD Guide for Challenging Disorganization: For Professional Organisers*. St Louis, MO: Institute for Challenging Disorganization.

International OCD Foundation. (2023). Is It Hoarding Disorder, Clutter, Collecting, or Squalor. Retrieved from https://hoarding.iocdf.org/about-hoarding/is-it-hoarding-clutter-collecting-or-squalor.

James, W. (1890). *The Principles of Psychology, Volume 1*. New York, NY: Henry Holt & Co.

Kahane, A. (2007). *Solving Tough Problems: An Open Way of Talking, Listening, and Creating New Realities*. Oakland, CA: Berrett-Koehler Publishers.

Kaizen™ Institute. (n.d.). What is KAIZEN™: Dive into the KAIZEN™ methodology. Retrieved from https://kaizen.com/what-is-kaizen.

Kellett, S. (2006). The treatment of compulsive hoarding with object-affect fusion informed CBT: Initial experimental case evidence. *Behavioural and Cognitive Psychotherapy*, 34(4), 481–485. doi: 10.1017/S1352465806003006.

Kellett, S. &. Knight, K. (2003). Does the concept of object-affect fusion refine cognitive-behavioural theories of hoarding? *British Association for Behavioural and Cognitive Psychotherapies*, 31(4), 457–461. doi: https://doi.org/10.1017/S1352465803004077.

Kim, H. J., Steketee, G. & Frost, R. O. (2001). Hoarding by elderly people. *Health and Social Work*, 26(3), 176–184. doi: https://doi.org/10.1093/hsw/26.3.176.

Kings, C. A., Moulding, R. & Knight, T. (2017, July). You are what you own: Reviewing the link between possessions, emotional attachment, and the self-concept in hoarding disorder. *Journal of Obsessive-Compulsive and Related Disorders, 14*, 51–58. doi: https://doi.org/10.1016/j.jocrd.2017.05.005.

Kolberg, J. (2007). *Conquering Chronic Disorganization*. Decateur, GA: Squall Press.

Kolberg, J. (2008). *What Every Professional Organizer Needs to Know About Chronic Disorganization*. Decateur, GA: Squall Press.

Kysow, K., Bratiotis, C., Lauster, N. & Woody, S. R. (2020). How can cities tackle hoarding? Examining an intervention program bringing together fire and health authorities in Vancouver. *Health Society Care Community, 28*(4), 1160–1169.

La Buissonnière-Ariza, V., Wood, J. J., Kendall, P. C. McBride, N. M. *et al.* (2018). Presentation and correlates of hoarding behaviors in children with autism spectrum disorders and comorbid anxiety or obsessive-compulsive symptoms. *Journal of Autism Development Disorders, 8*(12), 4167–4178. doi: 10.1007/s10803-018-3645-3.

Lally, P. (2010). How are habits formed: Modelling habit formation in the real world. *European Journal of Social Psychology, 40*(6), 998–1009. doi: https://doi.org/10.1002/ejsp.674.

Lally, P. & Gardner, B. (2013). Promoting habit formation. *Health Psychology Review, 7*(1), 137–158. doi: 10.1080/17437199.2011.603640.

LaMorte, W. W. (2022). The Transtheoretical Model (Stages of Change). Retrieved from Boston University School of Public Health: https://sphweb.bumc.bu.edu/otlt/mph-modules/sb/behavioralchangetheories/behavioralchangetheories6.html.

Lebow, H. I. (2022) Anxious Attachment Style: Signs, Causes, and How to Change: Causes of anxious attachment style. Retrieved from PsychCentral: https://psychcentral.com/health/anxious-attachment-style-signs#causes.

Limburg, K., Watson, H. J., Hagger, M. S. & Egan, S. J. (2017). The relationship between perfectionism and psychopathology: A meta-analysis. *Journal of Clinical Psychology, 73*(10), 1301–1326. doi: https://doi.org/10.1002/jclp.22435.

Lo, S. (ed.). (2022, October 23). What are pink and brown noise and how do they affect your brain? Retrieved from VeryWell Mind: www.verywellmind.com/exploring-the-potential-of-pink-and-brown-noise-for-neurodivergent-individuals-6751354.

Lumen. (2024). *Language and Thinking*. Retrieved from Lumen Learning: https://courses.lumenlearning.com/waymaker-psychology/chapter/reading-language-and-thought.

Macmillan, D. & Shaw, P. (1966). Senile breakdown in standards of personal and environmental cleanliness. *BMJ, 5521*(2), 1032–1037. doi: https://doi.org/10.1136/bmj.2.5521.1032.

Main, M. & Solomon, J. (1990). Procedures for Identifying Infants as Disorganized/Disoriented during the Ainsworth Strange Situation. In M. T. Greenberg, D. Cicchetti, & E. M. Cummings (eds), *Attachment in the Preschool Years: Theory, Research, and Intervention* (pp.121–160). Chilcago, IL: The University of Chicago Press.

Maslow, A. (1970). *Motivation and Personality*. New York, NY: Harper & Row.

McGlone, F. & Walker, S. (2021, May 17). Four health benefits of hugs – and why they feel so good. Retrieved from The Conversation: https://theconversation.com/four-health-benefits-of-hugs-and-why-they-feel-so-good-160935.

McInerney, S. J. (2002). Introducing the Biopsychosocial Model for good medicine and good doctors. *BMJ, 324*, 1537. doi: https://doi.org/10.1136/bmj.324.7353.1537/a.

Miller, W. R. & Rollnick, S. (2013). *Motivational Interviewing: Helping People Change* (third edition). New York, NY: Guilford Press.

Monzani, B., Rijsdijk, F., Harris, J. & Mataix-Cols, D. (2014). The structure of genetic and environmental risk factors for dimensional representations of DSM-5 obsessive-compulsive spectrum disorders. *JAMA Psychiatry, 71*(2), 182–189. doi: https://doi.org/10.1001/jamapsychiatry.2013.3524.

Muroff, J., Steketee, G., Rasmussen, J., Gibson, A., Bratiotis, C. & Sorrentino, C. (2009). Group cognitive and behavioral treatment for compulsive hoarding: A preliminary trial. *Depression and Anxiety, 26*(7), 634–640. doi: https://doi.org/10.1002/da.20591.

National Institute of Mental Health. (2021, January 14). NIMH expert Dr. Krystal Lewis discusses managing stress & anxiety. Retrieved from National Institute of Mental Health: www.nimh.nih.gov/news/media/2021/nimh-expert-dr-krystal-lewis-discusses-managing-stress-anxiety.

Neave, N., Tyson, H., McInnes, L. & Hamilton, C. (2016). The role of attachment style and anthropomorphism in predicting hoarding behaviours in a non-clinical sample. *Personality and Individual Differences, 99*, 33–37. doi: https://doi.org/10.1016/j.paid.2016.04.067.

Neziroglu, F. U.-P. (2020). The psychological, relational and social impact in adult offspring of parents with hoarding disorder. *Children Australia, 45*(3), 153–158. doi: https://doi.org/10.1017/cha.2020.42.

NHS. (2022, June 1). Hoarding Disorder. Retrieved from NHS UK: www.nhs.uk/mental-health/conditions/hoarding-disorder.

NHS Inform. (2023, April 4). Depression. Retrieved from NHS Inform: www.nhsinform.scot/illnesses-and-conditions/mental-health/depression#symptoms-and-causes-of-depression.

Nurses With Heart. (2023, April 4). The Illness of Everyone: Our Mental Health Crisis. Retrieved from https://nurseswithheart.com/home-health-care/anxiety/illness-everyone-mental-health-crisis.

Nutley, S. K., Read, M., Eichenbaum, J., Nosheny, R. L. *et al.* (2022, October). Poor sleep quality and daytime fatigue are associated with subjective but not objective cognitive functioning in clinically relevant hoarding. *Society of Biological Psychiatry, 2*, 480–488. doi: https://doi.org/10.1016/j.bpsgos.2021.10.009.

Patronek, G. J. (1999). Hoarding of animals: An under-recognized public health problem in a difficult-to-study population. *Public Health Report, 114*(1), 81–87. doi: 10.1093/phr/114.1.81.

Patronek, G. J. & Nathanson, J. N. (2009). A theoretical perspective to inform assessment and treatment strategies for animal hoarders. *Clinical Psychology Review, 29*(3), 274–281. doi: https://doi.org/10.1016/j.cpr.2009.01.006.

Postlethwaite, A., Kellett, S. & Mataix-Cols, D. (2019). Prevalence of hoarding disorder: A systematic review and meta-analysis. *Journal of Affective Disorders, 256*, 309–316. doi: https://doi.org/10.1016/j.jad.2019.06.004.

Prochaska, J. O. & DiClemente, C. C. (1982). Transtheoretical therapy: Toward a more integrative model of change. *Psychotherapy: Theory, Research and Practice*, 19(3), 276–288. doi: https://doi.org/10.1037/h0088437.

Prochaska, J. O., & DiClemente, C. C. (1983). Stages and processes of self-change of smoking: Toward an integrative model of change. *Journal of Consulting and Clinical Psychology*, 51(3), 390–395. doi: https://doi.org/10.1037/0022-006X.51.3.390.

Rasmussen, J. L., Brown, T. A., Steketee, G. S. & Barlow, D. H. (2013). Impulsivity in hoarding. *Journal of Obsessive-Compulsive and Related Disorders*, 2(2), 183–191. doi: https://doi.org/10.1016/j.jocrd.2013.02.004.

Reis, R. (2003). The Socratic method: What it is and how to use it in the classroom. Retrieved from Stanford University: https://web.archive.org/web/20220511021023/https://tomprof.stanford.edu/posting/810.

Reyes-Ortiz, C. A. (2001). Diogenes syndrome: The self-neglect elderly. *Comprehensive Therapy*, 27(117). doi: https://doi.org/10.1007/s12019-996-0005-6.

Richards, V. (2018, April 5). The importance of language in mental health care. *Lancet Psychiatry*, 5(6), 460–461. doi: 10.1016/S2215-0366(18)30042-7.

Richards, V. & Lloyd, K. (2017). *Core Values for Psychiatrists*. London: Royal College of Psychiatrists.

Richardson, J., Barker, L., Furness, J. & Simpson, M. (2014). *New Era, Changing Role for House Officers*. De Montfort University. Edinburgh: CIH & Wheatley Group.

Robertson, L., Paparo, J. & Wootton, B. M. (2020). Understanding barriers to treatment and treatment delivery preferences for individuals with symptoms of hoarding disorder: A preliminary study. *Journal of Obsessive-Compulsive and Related Disorders*, 26, 100560. doi: https://doi.org/10.1016/j.jocrd.2020.100560.

Rodriguez, C. I. & Frost, R. O. (2023). *Hoarding Disorder: A Comprehensive Clinical Guide* (first edition). Washington, DC: American Psychiatric Association.

Rogers, C. R. (1959). A Theory of Therapy, Personality, and Interpersonal Relationships: As Developed in the Client-Centered Framework. In S. Koch (ed.), *Psychology: A Study of a Science* (Volume 3) (pp.184–256). New York, NY: McGraw-Hill.

Rudge, C. (2018). Hoarding Ice-Breaker Form. Retrieved from https://hoardingicebreakerform.org.

Salama, A. & Alshuwaikhat, H. (2006). A trans-disciplinary approach for a comprehensive understanding of sustainable affordable housing. *Global Built Environment Review*, 5(3), 35–50.

Saldarriaga-Cantillo, A. & Rivas-Nieto, J. (2014). Noah syndrome: A variant of Diogenes syndrome accompanied by animal hoarding practices. *Journal of Elder Abuse and Neglect*, 27(3). doi: 10.1080/08946566.2014.978518.

Samuels, J. F. (2008). Prevalence and correlates of hoarding behavior in a community-based sample. *Behaviour Research and Therapy*, 46(7), 836–844.

Sanchez, C., Linkovski, O., van Roessel, P., Maayan Steinberg, N. *et al.* (2023, April). Early life stress in adults with hoarding disorder: A mixed methods study. *Journal of Obsessive-Compulsive and Related Disorders*, 37, 100785. doi: https://doi.org/10.1016/j.jocrd.2023.100785.

San Francisco Task Force on Compulsive Hoarding. (2009). *Beyond Overwhelmed*. Retrieved from www.mentalhealthsf.org/wp-content/uploads/2023/10/Task-Force-Report-FINAL.pdf.

Schwarzer, R. & Jerusalem, M. (1995). Generalized Self-Efficacy Scale. In J. Weinman, S. Wright & M. Johnston, *Measures in Health Psychology: A User's Portfolio. Causal and Control Beliefs* (pp.35–37). Windsor, UK: NFER-Nelson.

Scottish Fire and Rescue Service. (2024). Fire Fatality Analysis Report 2022-2023.

Scottish Government. (2022). Adult Support and Protection (Scotland) Act 2007: guidance for Adult Protection Committees. Retrieved from www.gov.scot/publications/adult-support-protection-scotland-act-2007-guidance-adult-protection-committees.

SERC. (2023). What Is Socratic Questioning. Retrieved from Science Education Resource Center: https://serc.carleton.edu/introgeo/socratic/second.html.

Shah, P. J. (2013). Adults with attention-deficit hyperactivity disorder – diagnosis or normality? *British Journal of Psychiatry*, 203(5), 317–319.

Shah, P. J. (2022). Neurodevelopmental disorders and neurodiversity: Definition of terms from Scotland's National Autism Implementation Team. *British Journal of Psychiatry*, 221(3), 577–579. doi: https://doi.org/10.1192/bjp.2022.43.

Singer, J. (1998). *Odd People In*. Sydney: University of Technology.

Singer, J. (1999). Why Can't You Be Normal For Once In Your Life? In M. Corker & S. French (eds.), *Disability Discourse*. Maidenhead: Open University Press.

Smith, M. M., Sherry, S. B., Vidovic, V., Saklofske, D. H., Stoeber, J. & Benoit, A. (2019). Perfectionism and the Five-Factor Model of Personality: A meta-analytic review. *Personality and Social Psychology Review: An Official Journal of the Society for Personality and Social Psychology*, 23(4), 367–390. doi: https://doi.org/10.1177/1088868318814973.

Steel, P. (2007). The nature of procrastination: A meta-analytic and theoretical review of quintessential self-regulatory failure. *Psychological Bulletin*, 133(1), 65–94. doi: https://doi.org/10.1037/0033-2909.133.1.65.

Steketee, G. & Bratiotis, C. (2020). *Hoarding – What Everyone Needs to Know*. New York, NY: Oxford University Press.

Steketee, G. & Frost, R. (2003, December 7). Compulsive hoarding: Current status of the research. *Clinical Psychology Review*, 23(7), 905–927. doi: https://doi.org/10.1016/j.cpr.2003.08.002.

Steketee, G. & Frost, R. O. (2013). *Treatment for Hoarding Disorder: Therapist Guide* (second edition). New York, NY: Oxford University Press.

Steketee, G. & Frost, R. O. (2014). *Treatment for Hoarding Disorder: Workbook* (second edition). New York, NY: Oxford University Press.

Stober, J. (1998). The Frost Multidimensional Perfectionism Scale: More perfect with four (instead of six) dimensions. *Personality and Individual Differences*, 24(4), 481–491. doi: https://doi.org/10.1016/S0191-8869(97)00207-9.

St-Pierre-Delorme, M.-E. & O'Connor, K. (2016). Using virtual reality in the inference-based treatment of compulsive hoarding. *Frontiers in Public Health*, 4, 149. doi: https://doi.org/10.3389/fpubh.2016.00149.

Toffler, A. (1970). *Future Shock*. New York, NY: Random House.

Tolin, D. F. (2023). Toward a biopsychosocial model of hoarding disorder. *Journal of Obsessive-Compulsive and Related Disorders, 36*, 100775. doi: https://doi.org/10.1016/j.jocrd.2022.100775.

Tolin, D. F., Frost, R. O. & Steketee, G. (2014). *Buried in Treasures: Help for Compulsive Acquiring, Saving, and Hoarding.* New York, NY: Oxford University Press.

Tolin, D. F., Frost, R. O., Steketee, G., Gray, K. D. & Fitch, K. E. (2008). The economic and social burden of compulsive hoarding. *Psychiatry Research, 160*(2), 200–211. doi: https://doi.org/10.1016/j.psychres.2007.08.008.

Tolin, D. F., Frost, R. O., Steketee, G. & Muroff, J. (2015). Cognitive behavioral therapy for hoarding disorder: A meta-analysis. *Depression and Anxiety, 32*(3), 158–166. doi: https://doi.org/10.1002/da.22327.

Tolin, D. F., Stevens, M. C., Villavicencio, A. L., Norberg, M. M. *et al.* (2012). Neural mechanisms of decision making in hoarding disorder. *Archives of General Psychiatry, 69*(8), 832–841. doi: https://doi.org/10.1001/archgenpsychiatry.2011.1980.

Tompkins, M. (2015a). Hoarding Behavior and Hoarding Disorder. In *Clinician's Guide to Severe Hoarding.* New York, NY: Springer.

Tompkins, M. A. (2015b). *Clinician's Guide to Severe Hoarding: A Harm Reduction Approach.* New York, NY: Springer.

Tompkins, M. A. & Hartl, T. L. (2009). *Digging Out: Helping Your Loved One Manage Clutter, Hoarding, and Compulsive Acquiring.* Oakland, CA: New Harbinger Publications.

Toyota Industries Corporation. (n.d.). The Story of Sakichi Toyoda. Retrieved from https://www.toyota-industries.com/company/history/toyoda_sakichi/index.html.

Vyskocilova, J., Prasko, J., Ociskova, M., Sedlackova, Z. *et al.* (2015). Values and values work in cognitive behavioral therapy. *European Psychiatry, 57*, 40–48. doi: 10.1016/j.eurpsy.2016.01.1660.

Wan, E. W. & Chen, R. P. (2021). Anthropomorphism and object attachment. *Current Opinion in Psychology, 39*, 88–93. doi: https://doi.org/10.1016/j.copsyc.2020.08.009.

Wang, Y. & Chiew, V. (2010). On the cognitive process of human problem solving. *Cognitive Systems Research, 11*(1), 81–92. doi: https://doi.org/10.1016/j.cogsys.2008.08.003.

Weir, K. (2020, April 1). Treating people with hoarding disorder. Retrieved from American Psychiatric Association: www.apa.org/monitor/2020/04/ce-corner-hoarding.

Whitmore, J. (1992). *Coaching for Performance: Growing Human Potential and Purpose – The Principles and Practice of Coaching and Leadership.* London: Nicholas Brealey Publishing.

Wilkinson, J., Schoultz, M., King, H., Neave, N. & Bailey, C. (2022). Animal hoarding cases in England: Implications for public health services. *Frontiers in Public Health, 10.* 899378. 10.3389/fpubh.2022.899378.

Woody, S. R., Kellman-McFarlane, K. & Welsted, A. (2014). Review of cognitive performance in hoarding disorder. *Clinical Psychology Review, 34*, 324–336. doi: http://dx.doi.org/10.1016/j.cpr.2014.04.002.

Woody, S. R., Lenkic, P., Neal, R. L. & Bogod, N. (2021). Neurocognitive functioning in hoarding disorder. *Journal of Obsessive-Compulsive and Related Disorders, 2211–3649.* doi: https://doi.org/10.1016/j.jocrd.2021.100658.

Wootton, B. M., Worden, B. L., Norberg, M. N., Grisham, J. R. & Steketee, G. (2019). A clinician's quick guide to evidence-based approaches: Hoarding disorder. *Clinical Psychologist, 23*(1), 85–87. doi: 10.1111/cp.12176.

World Health Organisation. (1986). The 1st International Conference on Health Promotion, Ottawa, 1986. Retrieved from www.who.int/teams/health-promotion/enhanced-wellbeing/first-global-conference.

World Health Organisation. (2018, June 18). WHO releases new International Classification of Diseases (ICD 11). Retrieved from www.who.int/news/item/18-06-2018-who-releases-new-international-classification-of-diseases-(icd-11).

World Health Organisation. (2023). WHO remains firmly committed to the principles set out in the preamble to the Constitution. Retrieved from www.who.int/about/governance/constitution.

Xiong, J., Lipsitz, O., Nasri, F., Lui, L. M. W. *et al.* (2020). Impact of COVID-19 pandemic on mental health in the general population: A systematic review. *Journal of Affective Disorders, 277*, 55–64. doi: https://doi.org/10.1016/j.jad.2020.08.001.

Subject Index

Author Index